How to Start a Home-Based
Housecleaning
Business

by Melinda Morse and Laura Jorstad

The
Globe
Pequot
Press

GUILFORD, CONNECTICUT

Cover design by Nancy Freeborn
Cover Photos by Peter Ardito, Index Stock; © PhotoDisc
Text Design by Mary Ballachino

Library of Congress Cataloging-in-Publication Data
Morse, Melinda.
    How to start a home-based housecleaning business / by Melinda Morse and Laura Jorstad. – 1st ed.
        p. cm. – (Home-based business series)
    Includes index.
    ISBN 0-7627-2226-6
    1. Building cleaning industry — United States — Management. 2. Home-based businesses — United States — Management. 3. New Business enterprises — United States — Management. 4. Small Business — United States — Management. 5. House cleaning — United States — Management. I. Title: Housecleaning business. II. Jorstad, Laura. III. Title IV. Series.

HD9999.B883 U655 2002
648'.5'0681—dc21   2002072679

Manufactured in the United States of America
First Edition/First Printing

Contents

Acknowledgments / vii

Introduction: Why a Home-Based Business? / ix

Chapter 1 Considering a Home-Based Housecleaning Business / 1

Starting a Business: The Reality / 1

Is a Home-Based Housecleaning Business Right for You? / 6

Chapter 2 Getting Started I: The Legalities / 11

What Kind of Business Am I? / 11

Choosing and Registering a Name for Your Company / 14

Applying for a Business License / 19

Setting Up a Business Bank Account / 22

Receiving Payments by Credit Card / 24

Chapter 3 Getting Started II: Getting Your Business off the Ground / 25

Setting Fees / 25

Learning from the Competition / 27

Getting the First Client or Two / 28

How to Get a Business Logo / 30

Chapter 4 How to Plan and Develop a Service Manual / 35

Presentation / 36

Cover Page / 36

Mission Statement / 36

The Consultation / 38

Clientele / 38

Services / 38

Confidentiality and Security / 39

Client Mailing List / 39

Safety / 40

Rates / 40

Scheduling / 41

Cancellations / 41

Billing and Payments / 42

Contract Renewal / 42

Community and Charitable Causes / 43

General Information / 43

Room Plans / 43

Sample Service Manual / 44

Chapter 5   How to Screen Clients / 65

By Telephone / 65

In Person / 66

Chapter 6   Cleaning 101 / 69

The Well-Stocked Cleaner / 69

A Cleaning Play-by-Play / 72

Scheduling / 75

Taking Care of Yourself / 77

Chapter 7   Understanding and Serving Customers / 81

Five Essential Elements of Customer Service / 83

Chapter 8   Setting Up the Home Office / 85

Basic Equipment / 85

Privacy / 90

Contents

Chapter 9   **Record Keeping** / 93

         Cash or Accrual? / 94

         The Business Checkbook / 94

         Mileage Records / 95

         Income Records / 95

         Expense Records / 95

         Monthly Net Income Statement / 98

         Client Records / 99

         Invoicing / 99

Chapter 10   **Taxes** / 103

         Deductions for the Home-Based Business / 103

         Deductions for the Housecleaning Business / 106

Chapter 11   **Insurance and Bonding** / 111

         Liability Insurance / 111

         Bonding / 117

Chapter 12   **Advertising** / 119

         The Web / 120

         Yellow Pages / 121

         Newspapers / 122

         Flyers / 123

         Business Cards / 124

         Magnetic Car Signs / 125

         Networking / 126

         Word of Mouth / 127

         Fund-raising and Community Outreach / 127

Contents

Chapter 13   When Bad Things Happen to Good Housecleaners   /   129

Chapter 14   The Future   /   133
Becoming an Employer /   133
Becoming a Specialist /   134

Appendix I   Checklist of Start-Up Requirements   /   137

Appendix II   Resources   /   138
Where to Get Your Business Questions Answered /   138
Where to Get Your Housecleaning Questions Answered /   140

Appendix III   Blank Room Plans   /   142

Index   /   163

About the Author   /   166

Acknowledgments

I wish to thank Byron Reese of PageWise Inc. for not hitting the delete button. A special thanks to small-business consultant Lisa Solari-Parravicini, and many thanks to Mary Norris of Globe Pequot Press.

—M. M.

Thanks to Jan Cronan, Liz Taylor, Mary Norris, and all the great folks at Globe Pequot Press. Karen Elliott did a thoughtful, meticulous edit. Special thanks to Linda Shelton and Nancy Manson, and to Mom, my anchor, role model, and best friend. I hope I'm just like you when I grow up.

—L. J.

Introduction: Why a Home-Based Business?

What is an entrepreneur? What does it take to be an entrepreneur? An entrepreneur is anyone who launches or manages a business venture, often assuming risks. Entrepreneurship is nothing new: Hyman Lipman, who in 1858 came up with the idea of placing rubber erasers on the ends of pencils, made $100,000 from the sale of the patent alone! Mary Kay Ash founded Mary Kay Cosmetics in 1963 with a $5,000 investment and turned it into a $2 billion company. And a half century before Mary Kay came Madam C. J. Walker, born Sarah Breedlove. The daughter of former slaves on a Louisiana plantation, this turn-of-the-twentieth-century washerwoman used $1.50—then a week's wages—to make the first batch of Wonderful Hair Grower, which she sold door to door. Her personal fortune at her time of death totaled some $2 million.

In the late 1980s the United States saw several workplace trends emerge, trends currently having a profound impact on twenty-first-century American workers. Jobs in corporate and industrial America, once considered secure, have been hit hard by cutbacks and downsizing. Not surprisingly, employee loyalty has fallen as well; according to the Bureau of Labor Statistics, the average worker holds 8.6 jobs between ages eighteen and thirty-two. Many people, too, are finding that a second and sometimes a third income is needed to make ends meet. With all this uncertainty—in a very uncertain world—now more than ever, people are investigating the possibilities of starting their own businesses to earn either a primary or a supplemental income. And many are based at home, more than 2 million a year, says *American Demographics* magazine.

Some examples of these home-based businesses are adventure tourism, bed-and-breakfasts, catering, event planning, interior design, landscaping, wedding consulting, and many, many more, including, of course, housecleaning! There's no limit to the possibilities for those who are creative, resourceful, and able to seize opportunities.

Most of the people who start home-based businesses are able to earn at least an extra income. Some entrepreneurs have been able to turn their endeavors into very profitable full-time careers. Not long ago the term *small business* brought to mind a little mom-and-pop corner store, or a one-person home-improvement provider who did the landscaping, the painting, and everything in between. Home-based workers were looked on with pity for failing to obtain *real* jobs. No more. Home-based entrepreneurs are now role models.

Family, friends, and neighbors seeking to do the same often approach these workers for advice. Small businesses are dynamic job creators, offering real opportunity for many who in the past had little access to economic power, as well as for those who want to take control of their own futures.

Indeed, small businesses are key to the economy of the United States, generating new opportunities for growth, which in turn creates new employment opportunities for diverse and underrepresented groups. Small businesses also help establish new products and innovative services in the current and future marketplace.

If the events of the twenty-first century have taught us anything, it is that things can change . . . fast. And in a world where what's here today could be gone in a heartbeat, there's a kind of security that comes from being self-sufficient. As an entrepreneur, you are in charge of your career and your life—not your boss, not company management, but you. You decide when and how much to work. You decide what fees to charge. When you work for yourself, no one can take your job away from you—ever. If things change in your life or your world, you can adapt your business right along with them. It's a different kind of safety net than you'll have at a corporate job, a kind that makes sense in the new millennium.

If you've ever considered starting a home-based business, now is the time to do it!

Chapter One

Considering a Home-Based Housecleaning Business

I f you're holding this book, put aside everything you have ever read or heard about starting a home-based business. For now, forget about investments, start-up costs, loans, and taxes. And especially forget about fancy vacations on cruise ships and impressing the neighbors with the latest-model SUV.

Starting a Business: The Reality

You've probably heard the fantasies sold by business start-up classes, seminars, Web sites, and infomercials: Starting a business requires only a few hours a day, and it is *so easy*. So easy that *anyone* can do it, and once you learn the *secrets*, you can instantaneously generate so much profit that within months, you'll be able to pay off your mortgage in full and travel around the world.

Here's the reality. Mass-marketed business start-up schemes conceal the three most basic components of any home-business ownership:

- Businesses are built, not created out of thin air.
- Business owners work harder for themselves than they ever did for anyone else.
- The single most important investment that you will make is to invest *yourself.*

Unless you've inherited a successful business, which is unlikely if you're reading this book, the first guiding principle is that all businesses are built from the ground up. To think otherwise is known in the business world as magical thinking, or the Lucky Charm illusion. You cannot buy formulas or secrets. Building a business requires more energy, stamina, commitment, and desire to get it right than does working for someone else, or for someone else's corporation. If working for yourself appeals to you, be prepared to work harder for yourself than you ever have for anyone else.

Many first-time business owners spend their life savings on advertising, equipment, services, and other products but soon go out of business because they never realized the truth about investing: The most important investment that you will ever make is to invest yourself.

Home-business start-ups end up in one of three ways:

1. They never get past the pondering or planning stage.
2. They fail because the business was not built from the bottom up. Too many beginning small-business owners will envision a five-story mansion and start to build the first floor. Somewhere around the stairs to the second floor, though, things begin to crumble. The owners forgot, ignored, or simply didn't know that they needed to lay a foundation before attempting to build from the ground up.
3. They succeed.

How do you make sure your business succeeds? You lay a foundation. The foundation is the plan behind why you are doing what you are doing, as well as a plan for where you are going. Without the foundation, you don't have a business.

If research, marketing, and physically working are not your cup of tea, then a home-based cleaning business isn't for you. Owning and operating a home-based business is no less work than any other professional career, whether as an attorney, a doctor, an accountant, or a plumber. It isn't an easy way to make money. It's not a get-rich-quick plot or a path to overnight success. Any successful home business is a progressive operation with an ongoing plan for working, improving the work, and profiting from that work.

That's the reality. But here's another truth: Becoming self-employed could be the best thing you'll ever do for yourself. Owning your own business can enable you to enjoy the pride, self-esteem, and sense of accomplishment that go along with having created something fulfilling that *works for you,* and that reflects your hard work and dedication. Not a lot of folks can say that about their careers.

Melinda's Story

When I started my housecleaning business I had about $80 in the bank. Everything else I learned and earned. The biggest investment that I made was to invest myself.

My background of abandoned career paths isn't much different from anyone else's story. As is the case with most people who are looking for job opportunities, or who are changing careers, the *why* comes before the *how*.

I didn't start my home-based cleaning business with any sort of business knowledge. I never even intended to start a business. I couldn't find a job to help me work my way through college, so I set out to create one. I thought it would be a temporary fix, something to pay bills until I was out of school. Yet in four years I managed to build and establish a successful home-based cleaning business that I am proud to say that I created, I built, I own, and I benefit from. By 1998 I was a successful entrepreneur and CEO with much more than $80 in the bank.

When I graduated from high school I had no idea what I wanted to do. I knew what I needed to do, and that was work. I never thought about employee benefits, investments, promotions, or job security. I started what I now call the *Job Habit*. I worked to maintain: to pay the rent, the car insurance, the utilities. There was never any money left over for vacations, savings, or those little fringe benefits like matching forks and spoons. Over the years I hopped from job to job in the hopes of encountering the Shangri-la that I'd heard so much about: a career with a corporation that would pay me enough money to have matching forks and spoons, and one that would also pay for my funeral. I didn't find it. Instead I was, like most people, one paycheck away from financial devastation, and I didn't think I had any marketable skills. I certainly didn't have $25,000 stashed away to invest in a business.

The idea of a career finally occured to me in my late twenties; in 1994 I decided to pursue my love for literature and haul myself off to college. My plan was to become an English teacher. Reading and writing were my first loves, and I thought that by teaching English, I would be able to read and write to my heart's content while at the same time turning on American's youth to the wonderful world of literature.

But I still needed to make ends meet while pursuing my plan. And finding part-time employment to correspond with my part-time class load was difficult. Moreover, my sort of enthusiasm was meaningless to employers who were looking for people to answer telephones or to punch keys on a cash register. The jobs I'd relied on as a younger person—salesclerk, temporary office administrative assignments, and a variety of entry-level positions at various companies—were no longer an option for me. Nobody said *You're too old*, but they didn't hire me.

I needed to find work and fast.

One afternoon at the post office, where I had just dumped off a pile of resumes that surely went into more than one round file, I ran into Ms. Weathers, the mother of a childhood acquaintance. I hadn't seen her in more than ten years. When she asked, "How are you?" I answered, "Not so good."

To my surprise, Ms. Weathers didn't just skip over my comment. She stopped and listened to me with heartfelt respect as I complained about the lack of part-time opportunities; about employers not returning phone calls or responding to resumes; about lying awake worrying that my car would be repossessed in the middle of the night. Then she told me she knew how I felt, because she'd been in my shoes. Ms. Weathers said in a proud voice, "That's why I clean houses." Over a good, long cup of coffee, she explained *her* plan.

Ms. Weathers had been a single mom for close to fifteen years. Her husband had died, leaving her without any savings or insurance benefits. There was a huge mortgage on the house, and she had no work experience other than a typing job she'd had as a teenager in the early 1960s. Yet she managed to put two children through college, keep on top of her mortgage, and still have money left for a car, a dog, and vacations twice a year.

I listened to her story, and felt a bit guilty for complaining about my so-called down-and-out life. Then Ms. Weathers suggested that I try to pick up a few housecleaning jobs, "just until you get on your feet." I told her that I'd think about it, even though I never thought I would.

Housecleaning?

Me?

No thanks.

I knew nothing about how to clean a house. In my own apartment, if paper towels and whatever bottle of spray cleaner was on sale that week didn't work, then whatever the stain was, it was going to stay there.

But later that evening I thought about Ms. Weathers. Somehow she was making it, and she had been for more than fifteen years. Perhaps it might be something I could do for a few months to catch up on the bills. I thought, *Well, how hard can it be?* I told myself I'd just follow the instructions on the backs of the cleaning fluid bottles.

I came up with scenarios in my head. I'd find elderly people who wanted a housecleaner because they were lonely and wouldn't notice or care if I missed a spot. Or I'd find a few rich bachelors who traveled all of the time and just wanted their furniture lightly dusted. Perhaps I'd find people who were handicapped and couldn't reach the tops of cabinets to dust them off.

I had a lot to learn.

And I did learn it—all too often the hard way. That's what this book is for. As you think about, make plans for, and then start up your own home-based housecleaning business, I hope my own experiences and hard-won knowledge can help you out. Maybe there are a few lessons you *won't* have to learn the hard way.

Let's get started.

Is a Home-Based Housecleaning Business Right for You?

There's one critical requirement if you're going to pursue a housecleaning business: You have to be in reasonably good health. This is a physical job; you'll be on your feet most of the day, bending, stooping, reaching, moving in sometimes unusual ways, and lifting occasionally heavy weights (and lots of light ones). It can add up to aches and pains by the end of the day for anyone, no matter what kind of shape you're in. That's why you need to take a realistic look at the state of your health and the kinds of physical demands you'll be facing before you begin. If you have chronic health issues that limit your ability to do certain things, you might need to reconsider your plans.

What else should you think about? As with any career, the more skills and talents you bring to your business, the better off you'll be. But one of the joys of owning your own business is that you can build it around your strengths and interests. If you're someone who thrives on routine, for instance, you might want to focus on finding a few good regular clients. If you like lots of variety, on the other hand, perhaps you can network with a caterer or party planner and focus on cleaning before or after special occasions.

What else should you think about? First of all, here are some things you *don't* have to be to thrive in a housecleaning career:

- **You don't have to be a great housekeeper yourself.** Sure, if your own home is a mess, your friends and family might tease you about it. The truth is, however, there is a difference between cleaning to suit yourself and cleaning to meet other people's needs. If you have a sense of professionalism—a strong desire to give your clients excellent service—you should do fine.
- **You don't have to be a "people person."** Shy people can thrive as housecleaners, al-

though if you're happiest working alone, there are some issues you'll want to consider. Running a housecleaning business *will* involve time with people. You have to sell your services to new clients, for instance, as well as greet the clients you work with when you arrive in their homes, deal with phone or e-mail inquiries, and so on. And you'll be on your own in these encounters; you won't have a boss or company behind you. Still, the essence of your business is the cleaning itself.

Marketing is probably the hardest part of the job for anyone, shy or not. And you have to do it; you can't clean for clients you don't have! The good news is that it gets easier over time. You get used to it, and you simply have more to talk about: You know what kinds of questions and concerns other clients have had, so you have a pretty good idea of what to say to potential customers. And once you have even a single client, you can focus on providing excellent service. That's the heart of your work; in the end, it's what will get you clients and keep them coming back. It doesn't matter if you're a party animal or utterly tongue-tied.

Yes, you have to be prepared for some people time, especially when your business is getting off the ground. If you can handle this, however, your people time will be balanced by plenty of independence and solitude as well.

- **You don't have to be a "quiet person" either.** If you thrive on contact with people, if conversations leave you energized and happy, you can build your business around these strengths too. Cleaning does involve a large amount of time spent working on your own, and you will have to deal with that, but you can find ways to build more interaction into your work. Focus on marketing, on networking with other entrepreneurs, on special-events cleaning. Be active in your community. Consider expanding your business by taking on employees.

Bottom line: A housecleaning business is what you make it. You'll spend a certain amount of time alone; you'll want to think about this—and your ability to be happy with it—realistically. Then build your business around what you love most.

So what qualities *should* you have to be a top-notch housecleaner? Here are a few that are important:

- **Hardworking.** Owning a business is very hard work, and owning a housecleaning

Top Ten Reasons to Be a Housecleaner

1. Immediate gratification. Walk in and a house is dirty. Walk out and it's sparkling clean. That's a good feeling.
2. Meeting people's needs. Not only can you enjoy your own satisfaction at a clean house, but you can also know that your clients are enjoying it!
3. Setting your own hours. To a large degree, you can tailor your schedule to meet your needs. Want to be home when the kids get out of school? Arrange for it.
4. Choosing whom you work for and when. If a prospective client makes you uncomfortable, you can simply turn the job down.
5. Meeting new people. You'll meet all sorts of people in this job, from every walk of life, including some you might otherwise never get to know.
6. Variety. No two days are ever the same.
7. Pride. Here's a chance to be the very best you can be—in a business that you own.
8. Tax breaks. You may be able to deduct many of your expenses from your tax bill (see chapter 10).
9. Minimal start-up cost. The more seed money you have, the better (naturally!), but you can in fact get started in this business for the cost of transportation to your first client's home.
10. Profits! You can make a good living cleaning houses—and some people make a *great* living.

business is even harder. Are you ready to give up free time to do administrative work or to distribute flyers door to door? Will you want to spend evenings or weekends answering phone inquiries or giving estimates? Make sure you have a realistic picture of what business ownership will be like before you leap in.

• **Disciplined.** You don't get sick days in this business (at least not paid ones), and you don't get paid vacations or personal time either. If you don't show up, you don't get paid—and you lose clients fast. As a service provider, living up to your commitments is your job description. Do it and you'll succeed. Don't and you won't.

• **Conscientious.** Clients may have different cleaning standards than you do, and you have to meet them. If you walk into a room that looks like you could perform surgery in it, would you blow off cleaning it, or would you roll up your sleeves and get to work, because that's your job? If it's the end of the day and you're beat, would you take a few shortcuts cleaning that kitchen, or would you buckle down and give it the full treatment? Clients may never notice all the things you do clean, but they sure will notice everything you *don't* do.

• **Able to keep a secret.** You will—trust me—learn a lot of secrets about people on this job. It's critical that you keep these to yourself. If your clients don't trust you, you don't have a business.

That said, there are some secrets that shouldn't be ignored, and you'll want to consider getting outside help to deal with them. Domestic abuse, child abuse, drug abuse, criminal activity—it's unlikely that you'll confront any of these, but it is possible. Be prepared to face some complicated and difficult decisions. (Just don't face them alone. Get the advice of someone you trust.)

• **Personal boundaries.** This will help you out a lot. As an entrepreneur, you'll be sacrificing a lot of your time and energy—but save some for yourself. It's important to know how to say "no." Know what kinds of behavior are acceptable to you and what kinds aren't. Don't expect your clients to be your friends. (For more about boundaries, see chapter 13.)

• **Support system.** Any business can be a lonely, scary venture, not to mention exhausting, frustrating, discouraging, and, yes, sometimes exhilarating too. The more people you have around to share all these emotions with, the better off you'll be. Having the support of your spouse and children can make or break a business, and there's no substitute for a network of friends to listen, encourage, commiserate, celebrate, and give foot rubs.

If you're lacking in the support department—recently divorced, or new to an area, for example—see chapter 6 for some ideas about how to help take care of yourself.

Chapter Two
Getting Started I: The Legalities

S o you've decided that a home-based housecleaning business is right for you—congratulations! It's time now to build the foundation for your new business. And that starts with understanding and following the legal requirements for your operations.

Although you might be a micro enterprise, this doesn't mean that your business is at any time exempt from following government rules and regulations when it comes to forming, operating, and paying taxes on your home business.

The first step is usually applying for a business name and license. Before you can do this, however, there's another decision for you to make.

What Kind of Business Am I?

There's more than one way to own a business. Before applying for a license, you must be clear on your business's type of ownership. The designation usually depends on the type of service or product being offered. Most small home-based businesses are sole proprietorships. Other types of businesses are corporations, partnerships, and limited liability companies (LLCs).

In most cases, a sole proprietorship is appropriate for a home-based cleaning business. Being a sole proprietor simply means that you are the owner of the business, and that you aren't entering into a partnership or corporation. These terms can be confusing if you're not familiar with them, so here are the basics.

Sole Proprietor

A sole proprietorship is a structure that identifies you as legally doing business. In a sole proprietorship, federal and state income tax laws view you and your business as one entity. The business can only be owned by you (although in some states a sole proprietorship can be extended to include a spouse). For a one-person business that does not generate more than a million dollars a year, a sole proprietorship makes the most sense.

A sole proprietorship is also the most inexpensive type of business to start up. Your business taxes are paid through the personal income taxes that you file at year end. Any losses that you have suffered as a sole proprietor can be deducted from your annual income tax. The business and personal taxes are calculated at the same rate. Your business earnings are considered to be your personal earnings, so the more prosperous your business, the higher the rate of personal taxation. That's not a bad thing! Consider that if you worked for a corporation and earned $50,000 a year, you'd be in a higher tax bracket than if you earned $50,000 in profits from a home business. This is because as a business owner, you'll be making plenty of itemized tax deductions, so your overall profit and bottom line will be lower than if you earned the same salary working for someone else. (There's more on taxes in chapter 10.)

The downside is that if you can't pay debts that were incurred as operational expenses for your business, or if your business fails, not only will your business assets be at stake, but your personal assets can also be seized to pay off the debts. Personal assets include property such as real estate, as well as belongings such as a coin collection. If the sole proprietor dies, the business dies with her or him. Many new business owners worry about losses that might be accrued in the wake of a lawsuit. This shouldn't be an issue for you, however; you can purchase liability insurance to cover you in the case of lawsuits, even up to a million dollars. (See chapter 11 for more on insurance.) You can rest assured that your property will not be seized if you ruin someone's kitchen sink.

Corporation

Corporations are very complicated, and forming one is costly. The general difference between a sole proprietorship and a corporation is that a corporation has a lot more money at risk, so it must exist as a legal entity separate from its owner. In doing so, the corporation gains a few advantages, but at a heavy cost. For example, a profitable corporation would be able to issue company stock. The selling and trading of stock is regulated by the Internal Revenue Service as well as at the state level, so simply getting the go-ahead to trade stocks could cost the corporation hundreds of thousands of dollars.

In another instance, should a corporation be sued—say, in a class-action lawsuit—the owner would be protected from liens that might otherwise be placed against her or his personal property. It is unlikely that a small home business would ever generate enough profit (we're talking in the million-dollar range) to sell stock or to worry about a class-action lawsuit. On the other hand, no one person in a corporation can be held liable for business debts or actions. If an owner dies, the corporation is not affected. In the case of a corporate bankruptcy, business assets can be seized, but not personal property or assets. Depending on the scope of the business, a corporation can seek either federal or state incorporation. Incorporating requires a lawyer, and the accompanying hefty legal fees.

Partnership

In this ownership structure, you legally partner with at least one other person to conduct the business as co-owners. All parties are seen as equal and responsible entities. They equally share the business losses and liabilities as well as the profits. Each partner pays business income taxes in relation to her or his specific percentage share in the business. Partnerships can be financially advantageous for larger enterprises, because each partner represents a funding source: the more partners, the more start-up funds. Also, each partner brings a set of individual skills and experiences to the company; each one has something different to offer the business.

If the business suffers losses because of one partner, all partners will have to deal with the consequences. If a partner dies or drops out of the partnership, or if a new partner joins, then the existing partnership will dissolve and a new one must be formed. A great amount of trust is needed in order for a partnership to succeed.

All too often, partnerships have been the cause of irreconcilable differences, ending in the dissolution of the structure; this is particularly true when family members and friends venture into a partnership. Partnerships can be a legal nightmare. We don't recommend that you ever form a legal partnership for a new business. You're setting yourself up for heaps of trouble when it comes to dissolving the partnership, or even for simple day-to-day operations. In a worst-case scenario, your partner could disappear with the entire bank account, leaving you responsible for the business.

Limited Liability Company (LLC)

LLCs are very complicated and rarely found in a home-business environment. The limited liability company partially protects the business owner by limiting the amount of money and property that the company might lose through lawsuits or bankruptcy. Often the liability is limited to the amount of the investment in the company, and the rules are even more complicated when it comes to the investments of other partners and investors. An LLC would not be an option for a housecleaning business, because you aren't investing hundreds of thousands of dollars, and it's unlikely that you'd ever be sued for an amount that exceeds your insurance liability. Also, having one or more partners with large investments would be unlikely. An LLC would be more appropriate for a company that provided financial services with global dealings.

Choosing and Registering a Name for Your Company

Deciding on a name for your company isn't as easy as it sounds—most of the unique, catchy names are already taken. Your best bet is to choose three or four names that you like and that reflect a positive image, a first choice and two or three others that you can live with. Then if your top choice is already in use by someone else, you'll have one or more to fall back on. Here's a tip that will save you a lot of time and trouble when it comes to registering your company's name: Use your last name as part of the company name. This probably won't work as well if your last name is common, such as Jones or Smith. If your last name is unusual, however—say, Smitheron—try something like Smitheron Cleaning. A company that uses the owner's name is less likely to be in use, and it will be easier for people to find your company in the phone book or on the Internet if all they can remember is your last name.

Avoid using generic, clichéd names: Super Cleaners, Kleen Cleaners, Elite Cleaning, Quality Cleaners, and so forth. These names are a dime a dozen, and in no way will they allow you or your company to stand out from among the scores of other companies with similar names. Choosing a common and overused name could even cause you to lose business to companies with similar names. Clients who can't remember that you are Elite Cleaning Service might phone Executive Elite Cleaning Services, someone else's company.

We've never liked the use of the word *maid* in association with housecleaning. Maids are full-service employees, and provide more than the general housecleaning services. If you do include *maid* in your name, you're likely to receive tons of calls for cooking, catering services, and child care or nanny services. Stick to a company name and titles that represent what you are: a housecleaner.

Poor Name Choices:
> Progress Cleaners
> Prompt Cleaners
> Clean and Go
> Sparkle Cleaners
> Executive Maid Service

Great Examples of Simple Names:
> Cornerstone Cleaning (it's simple yet elegant)
> Boiling Kettle Cleaning Service (boiling kettle, clean water—nice analogy)
> Rags and Roses Cleaners (we can smell the roses, can't you?)
> The Cleaning Agents (the X-Files of housecleaning!)
> SOS Cleaning (the call for help, SOS, is whimsical, but not too cute)

Once you've come up with a couple of possibilities, what's next? You need to be sure that no one else is using the name you've chosen. There are a few ways to do this. The easiest is to go to the county clerk's office and review the local deed registry to determine whether anyone within your city or town is using the name. You can also do a name search at most libraries. The fee is usually between $5.00 and $15.00 for a search. If you're using your last name as part of the company's name, and the last name isn't too common, there's a good chance that no one else is using it. Once you've cleared the name at the local registry, you can register your name at the county level; there may be an additional small fee. This means that no one else can come along and legally use your company's name.

The next step is to proceed to the state level. Here, the secretary of state's office takes care of state business name searches and registration; the fee for name searches in most states is between $10 and $15. Once you receive documentation that the name is not being used, you can file for state registration. (Again, a fee may be charged.) The name is then yours to use. Most people stop registering at the state level. Because your cleaning business is a local business, and not one in which you're shipping products or retailing items worldwide, there really is no reason to patent or trademark the name. However, you do want to be sure that you are not infringing on someone else's trademark.

If you want to register "Tompkins' Cleaning Crew" in Utah and both the local and state searches turn up clear, you also want to do a search with the Patent and Trademark Office (PTO) located in Washington, D.C. You can get the forms by mail or on the Web site (www.uspto.gov); most libraries can also provide you with either the paperwork or a full-service search. If the PTO search reveals that the name Tompkins' Cleaning Crew is patented by someone in Massachusetts, you cannot legally use the name. That would be like opening up a hamburger stand and calling it McDonald's Burgers (even if your last name is McDonald).

Patents and trademarks are not common in sole proprietorships. They're expensive to file, the paperwork can be exhausting, and they usually require an attorney's intervention, so most people don't bother. As long as you aren't infringing on someone's trademark, I wouldn't worry about getting a patent on your own business name. In the United States there may be 11,000 companies with the name Tompkins' Cleaning Crew. Providing none of these companies is doing business in your town or the next county, it's perfectly fine for all of you to coexist without having to worry about patent or trademark infringement—if, that is, no one has applied for and received a patented trademark for the business use of the name.

The next step is to file for a fictitious business name. This sounds a bit frightening, but it takes less than fifteen minutes and costs between $10 and $50. It is required if you're doing business using any name other than your own. Some people deliberately keep their entire name as the name of the business in order to avoid having to file for a fictitious business name. For example, a sole proprietorship named Joe Normandy would not have to file as a fictitious business because Joe Normandy is not fictitious. Joe Normandy's Cleaning Company, however, would have to file a fictitious business name registration because, of

Sample Fictitious Name Registration Form

1. The name as you wish it to be registered:

   _____

2. A brief statement of the character or nature of the business or other activity to be carried on under or through the fictitious name:

   _____

   _____

   _____

3. The mailing address of the business (this address does not have to be the principal place of business and can be directed to anyone's attention):

   _____

   _____

4. The county where the principal place of business of the fictitious name is located. If there is more than one county, list all applicable counties or state "multiple":

   _____

   _____

5. Federal Employer Identification (FEI) number if known or if applicable:

   _____

6. Owner's name, address, and Social Security number (the Social Security number is not mandatory):

   _____

   _____

   _____

   _____   _____
   Owner's signature   Daytime telephone number:

course, there's no person named Joe Normandy's Cleaning Company. The problem with simply using your full name, however, is this: Who would make the connection between Joe Normandy and a cleaning business? Using a full name might work for a restaurant or an artist, but not in the cleaning industry. Without mentioning cleaning or cleaners in conjunction with your last name, clients will have no idea what sort of service you provide.

Filing for a fictitious business name serves several purposes. For one, it establishes you as a community business. Once you file, you are required to place an ad in a local newspaper to announce your DBA (doing business as). This is a practice dating back to colonial times. In the colonial era, tradesmen (women were not allowed to own businesses) and artisans often had similar names and trades that made it impossible to discern who owned which business. For example, there could have been forty-two blacksmiths named John Brown who lived in colonial Boston. Placing a newspaper statement would clarify which John Brown, residing at which address, owned the blacksmith shop on 12th Street.

The newspaper ad as well as the actual on-file fictitious business name document make it easy for people to find you, the owner of the company. In general, the only people who *need* to find you would be customers who wish to lodge a complaint against an unknown company owner, or those wishing to obtain your mailing address so that they can bombard you with investment opportunities and sales pitches. A fictitious business name document is freely available to the public. Consider also that a person wishing to open a business using the same name as yours—say, Sunshine Cleaning Service—will have the right to do so if you haven't registered the name.

The second purpose of the fictitious business name document is that it's required in order to open a business bank account, as well as to maintain business accounts for credit or invoicing. Without the document, most banks will refuse to open an account, while some may open the account but place a hold on it until they have received a copy of the document. Or worst of all, the bank will open a business account for you without the document, and you'll have no trouble for years, until you receive a letter from the bank stating that your account is frozen because it was discovered that your file is missing a copy of your fictitious name registration document. It will take you weeks to file and receive the document in order to regain control of your bank account. And that's assuming that in the years since you started your business, no one else has come along and filed a fictitious name document that uses the same name as your business! Remember also that many stores and on-line retailers in the cleaning industry will open a business credit account for you, enabling you to purchase supplies at a generous discount. To prevent misrepresentation, the companies will require your fictitious name registration number. You can't afford not to have the document when it comes to discounted supplies.

The third and most important function of the document is that you have no legal standing without it. For example, let's say that you are John Jones, the owner of Sunshine Cleaning Services. Two months ago, a client responded to a Sunshine Cleaning Service business card that you posted in the supermarket. You rendered service to the client, and left a bill. You did not receive a check in the mail, so you billed the client again, and again. The client ignored subsequent bills and telephone calls. You decide to take the client to small claims court to recoup your fee, plus late charges. You fill out the appropriate papers at the courthouse and pay the filing fee. The clerk asks for your fictitious name registration form or number. You don't have one. You're out of luck. In the court's eyes, Sunshine Cleaners performed the service, and Sunshine Cleaners, not John Jones, is the payee for the service. Therefore, Sunshine Cleaners is the only entity that can file a claim and bring the nonpaying client to court, and in the court's view, Sunshine Cleaners doesn't exist. You don't want to be met with a situation like this.

Applying for a Business License

With your ownership decided and your name registered, you're ready to receive a business license. The legal criteria for these licenses vary from state to state, county to county, city to city. Check with your local county clerk for information specific to your locality. As the owner of a business, you must comply with all federal, state, and local regulations. You must also register your business in order to file tax documents. Without the proper license and registration, you are not a legitimate business, and therefore not entitled to any of the federal or state tax opportunities.

Unfortunately, obtaining a license is where many housecleaning businesses fall short. This is where professionals are separated from the work-for-cash sorts of operations. If anything were to happen—such as a lawsuit—and it was discovered that you were operating an unlicensed business, you'd be setting yourself up for some pretty hefty fines as well as embarrassment.

Sole proprietorships are relatively easy to register and license. Difficulties occur only when the sole proprietor is retailing a product such as food or clothing, or when a regulated service such as child care or hairstyling is involved. Housecleaning services are not regulated, and you are not retailing regulated products or services, so the process is fairly simple.

Remember, a business license only allows you to legally operate a business within a specified locale; it does not license you as housecleaner. Sometimes clients will see the term *licensed* on your business card and misinterpret it as meaning that you're certified by an accrediting source to perform the duties of a housecleaner. Some vocational trades do require job-specific certification at the state level. For example, in addition to registering and licensing as a business, hairstylists and electricians must pass a written exam to obtain a license to practice trade. There are no accrediting sources for housecleaners—although you will find some cleaning personnel who work within major chemical industry facilities, such as a chemical treatment plant or hazardous waste facility, who've received college degrees and certifications in sanitation and waste management. Let's hope that you can stick to cleaning soap scum and window grime; hazardous waste cleaning is dangerous!

Some states' license applications are ten pages long, while those from other states are only a half page. The two most important questions on the application are about what type of business you're licensing and where you intend to do business.

In most cities and states, you can register a sole proprietorship for less than $250 a year. In New Mexico the cost is $35 a year. In Pennsylvania the cost is $200, but the license is good for a lifetime. Following are some common questions about business licenses.

Do I need a business license even if my business is home based and I have no employees?

Yes. All persons conducting a business must register a sole proprietor business license application.

Do I need a license even if I'm doing business simply under my own name?

If you're simply cleaning under your own name, you usually don't need a license, but this varies from locale to locale, so you'll want to check. But you're much better off doing business under a business name. Take the time to register your business; it's worth it.

Sample Business License Application

Name: _____

E-mail address: _____

Business Information

Name of business: _____

Mailing address: _____

Property address: _____

Telephone numbers: _____

Federal employer tax ID number: _____

State sales tax ID number: _____

Type of ownership: _____

State registration/license number: _____

Number of employees: _____

Type of business (please describe *in detail* products and services provided): _____
_____
_____

If a professional license is required, list the license type, license number, name of license holder, and his or her position in the business: _____
_____
_____

Does this business export a product or service to a foreign country? _____

Do you sell tobacco products as a retailer? _____

Owner Information

Owner 1 name: _____

Address: _____

Owner 2 name: _____

Address: _____

Emergency Contacts

Names and telephone numbers of people (managers, key holders) to contact in case of an emergency (such as fire or robbery)

Name: _____

Telephone: _____

Name: _____

Telephone: _____

Name: _____

Telephone: _____

Do I need a license from my state, county, **and** *city?*

Procedures vary around the country; you'll have to do the research about your own location. Start with your town or county clerk, or with a librarian. The Small Business Administration is also a good place to turn to for information and help on licensing; see Resources in the back of this book.

Where am I permitted to do business?

Some states have zoning policies that will not allow you to do business outside of the jurisdiction of certain counties and townships without applying for separate licenses. Most states do not. For those states that require multiple licensure for adjacent areas, the fees are generally low: between $15 and $100.

Setting Up a Business Bank Account

In the past, banks made it very difficult for small businesses to maintain a checking or savings account. Only a few years ago, it was common for small-business owners to ask clients to make checks payable to the owner rather than to the business. Who could have blamed them, when banks were charging inflated fees simply to deposit a single check?

Happily, those days are gone. Today most small-business accounts come with a variety of options for fees and account maintenance. Still, business accounts are nowhere near as flexible as personal accounts. You'll want to research several banks to find one that meets your needs, with low costs and no hidden fees.

While you're comparison shopping, it's a good idea to find out whether a bank can offer you a merchant credit card account in addition to your business account. A merchant account would allow clients to pay with a credit card. If you're planning to offer this payment option to clients—now or in the future—it can be a real convenience to do so through a single bank. There's more about merchant accounts later in this chapter.

Bank Shopping

When comparing banks' business account rates, a new proprietor of a service-oriented business is likely to think, *I don't need a checking account, because I'm not going to write checks from the account.* Although it's true that you might never write a single check from a business checking account. it's still the best way to go. It's inexpensive to maintain, and you don't need to order boxes of checks—you won't need them.

One of the best ways to keep fees to a minimum is to query the bank where you currently hold your personal accounts. If you're already a customer in good standing, most banks will allow you to open a business checking account and link it to your personal checking or savings account. This way, you need only make deposits into your business account and then transfer funds once or twice a month from the business account into your personal account. Many banks now offer the option of transferring funds and accessing your accounts on-line.

Remember to keep personal and business-related banking separate. Use your business account only for your business.

Business Account Paperwork

Most of the low-fee business accounts out there are simplified checking accounts. A simplified business checking account is generally used for a sole proprietorship that deposits fewer than a hundred items per month, and has no complicated business dealings such as tax liens, letters of credit requesting high escrow, or questionable international transactions. You should know that over the past decade or so, simple business checking accounts have been used by illegal money laundering operations, so don't be offended if a bank representative asks you, "What is the nature of your business?" The representative is required by federal law to ask, as well as to keep a written record of your answer.

When you open the account, you're opening it as a sole proprietorship with a DBA (doing business as)—your fictitious business name statement. Not all banks require the documentation, but it's a good idea to get the DBA before making a trip to the bank. By doing so, you won't be in for any surprises, and you'll appear as an organized, professional business owner.

In most states, a sole proprietor uses her or his Social Security number to serve as the employer identification number (EIN). When you file income tax, you and your business are one and the same. Thus you can deduct your business losses against your total household income.

Most simple business checking accounts require a small minimum balance—usually between $100 and $250—and are usually non-interest-bearing. So you'll want to develop a schedule to transfer the funds from the non-interest-bearing business account into an interest-bearing account, such as your personal savings account. The sooner you can transfer the funds to an interest-bearing account, the more money you'll be able to save. Be careful not to exceed your monthly transaction limit. Transaction limits range from seventy-five to one hundred, and the transfer of funds to another account is indeed counted as a transaction.

Here are a couple of examples of typical business account structures. What you find at your bank may, of course, be different.

Account Example 1

Monthly fee (waived with minimum balance) $12
Minimum average daily balance to waive monthly fee $7,500
Line of credit overdraft protection? . . . . No
Savings overdraft protection? . . . . Yes
Fee per transaction . . . . $1.00 after the first 75
transactions per month

Account Example 2

Monthly fee (waived with minimum balance) $25
Minimum average daily balance to waive monthly fee $100
Line of credit overdraft protection? . . . . No
Savings overdraft protection? . . . . Yes
Fee per transaction . . . . $0.25 after the first 100
transactions per month

Receiving Payments by Credit Card

Many financial institutions offer something called merchant accounts, which allow you to accept payment by credit card. The application process is fairly simple and straightforward. You'll want to shop around, however, because different banks offer different terms. Ask about each bank's fees, including per-item fees, supply fees, and statement fees. Make sure you understand the process thoroughly, and know who to contact in case of problems or questions.

Chapter Three

Getting Started II: Getting Your Business off the Ground

The scariest part of a business is getting started. How do you find the clients? How do you provide referrals if you're just starting out? How do you set fees that are comparable to those of your competitors? It's enough to send you running for the Pepto-Bismol! Still, taking it one step at a time, along with being highly organized, will get you moving in the right direction in no time.

Setting Fees

Fee setting is tricky—for housecleaning and for any service. If you ever need a room in your home painted, for instance, you can call dozens of painters, all of whom will give you a different price. You might receive estimates ranging from $150 to $1,200 for the same labor and supplies. Some painters will price their assignments by the hour, and some by the job. One hourly painter might charge $30 while another charges $200. Housecleaning businesses are similar: Some charge by the assignment, and some by the hour. Some even charge by the quarter hour. You'll find that one cleaner charges $50 for a four-hour job, while another charges $150.

Why such extreme fluctuations? One reason is that many housecleaning businesses operate with several employees. With each employee comes increased expenses for liability insurance, bonding, transportation reimbursement, cell phones, and so forth. In order for the proprietor to turn a profit, the client charges have to more than adequately cover expenses.

Expanding your business by adding employees thus isn't always a wise business choice. While a multistaffed cleaning business might charge $150 to clean a six-room home, a sole proprietor could charge $75 for the same job. If your services are priced out of range, clients will balk at hiring you. A wise consumer would look for services that fall somewhere in the middle price range. Goods or services that cost more aren't necessarily better.

The first step in fee setting is to have a realistic estimate of your actual expenses, including insurance, licensure, supplies, equipment, advertising, and so on. If your fees don't cover your expenses, you're obviously going to have problems, and fast! Use the monthly expense record in chapter 9 to estimate your own expenses for three months. Be as accurate and realistic as you can; wherever possible, do the research and plug in the actual expense amounts (for licenses, insurance and bonding policies, and the like), not just estimates. Once you have an idea of how much money you'll be spending to stay in business, you'll have a beginning point from which to calculate your fees.

Many other factors go into fee setting besides expenses, including the needs of your specific locale. The prices of goods and services in cities and areas with large populations are higher than in areas with smaller populations where there's less demand for the same goods and services. If you live in a rural area, take driving distances into consideration. Will you need to drive long distances to get to clients' homes? Do the clients live on the opposite ends of town? If you're servicing two clients on the same day, does it take you forty minutes or longer to get from the home of client A to the home of client B? If you'll be spending three hours a day driving, then your fees must adequately compensate you for those hours.

How much competition do you have? Are you finding that you have to drive to the next county in order to secure clients at all? Or are people snapping up your service like hotcakes? Are you utterly exhausted at the end of the day, with little profit to show for it? It takes time and experience in order to know exactly what sort of fees will bring the best results. Rest assured that you will gain the experience, and in no time you'll feel like an old pro!

Here's one last piece of advice: Don't be afraid to charge the fees you deserve. Yes, you might want to start on the lower end if you're new to the business, then raise your fees as you gain experience. But don't undersell yourself. You will work very hard as a house-cleaner, and what you do is important to your clients. You *are* worth the money you charge!

Learning from the Competition

Get to know your competitors: who they are, what they do, and what they charge. Gather information from all possible advertising venues: newspapers, yellow pages, business cards from bulletin boards, flyers that have been posted at the supermarket, Web sites, and so on. You should be able to come up with a list of all the housecleaning service providers in your immediate area.

On a card, record the name, telephone number, and Internet address of fifteen or so of the businesses, as well as the name and title of the contact person. Visit the companies' Web sites, and then spend an afternoon calling these businesses. Posing as a potential customer, get as much information as you can without raising suspicion. The businesses are open to the public, and anyone has the right to make a simple inquiry. Ask the following questions and record the answers on your index cards:

- **How soon could I obtain an estimate for housecleaning?** Is the next appointment for an estimate six months away or next Friday?
- **Do you charge by the hour, or by the job?** If hourly, what is the rate? Service providers who charge by the hour get their hourly wage whether the job was completed or not.
- **Is there a minimum number of hours required?** Most housecleaners will require at least two hours.
- **How are routine visits scheduled?** Perhaps the company serves the north end of the city on Mondays and Tuesdays, or perhaps apartments are done on Thursdays and Fridays while large homes are done only on Wednesdays and Thursdays.
- **Do you serve my area?** If not, what is the zone of service? Will the company accommodate potential out-of-zone clients for an added fee?
- **Are you insured and bonded?** Ask for the name of the provider and an account number so that you can phone to confirm the information.
- **How long have you been in business?**

- **Do you offer written information about your services, procedures, and policies?**
- **What are the payment options?**
- **Do you have employees or does the owner complete the assignments?** If there are employees, are they insured and bonded as well? How long have the employees been with the company?

If the person says that she or he will call you back, or will e-mail you with answers, and doesn't, be sure to note that on your card too. Get a sense of how you were treated. Did the person seem bored or irritated that you called or wrote? If the person spoke to you in a gruff or frustrated tone, then perhaps business isn't going well—or maybe it's going *too* well. A negative impression could indicate problems with the service, and you need to record this on the index card. There may come a time when you're overloaded with business and need to network with other housecleaners to exchange client referrals. You certainly don't want to refer an inappropriate service provider to a potential client!

Don't discount someone who won't disclose information on the telephone, but prefers to do an in-home consultation prior to discussing rates and availability. Insisting on an in-home consultation or estimate is the sign of an organized and professional housecleaner. Although you won't be able to get the information without a consultation, you'll at least have an idea of the sorts of professionals you will be competing with.

Be aware too that proprietors may be justifiably nervous about disclosing information if they sense you're a competitor. You really can't ask someone to spill the tricks of the trade so that you can then offer the same services for a reduced price. That's called undercutting, and it's unethical. So be professional, and gather whatever information you can by telephone or on-line. You'll get a pretty good idea of what others are doing and how they are doing it. But do use the information responsibly.

Getting the First Client or Two

When you go out for your first consultation, the potential client will inevitably want to know the extent of your experience, how long you've been in business, and how many clients you currently serve. Few people want to be the first client.

So how do you round up enough experience so that the first potential client doesn't feel like an experiment? There are a couple of ways to do this.

Volunteer to Clean the Home of a Friend or Family Member

Friends and family members are your best resources! Perhaps someone in your circle of friends or relatives has recently had a baby, or has taken a new job with long hours, or is overwhelmed with night classes and a heavy daytime schedule. Offer to give the person a break by doing some free housecleaning. Explain that you're building up clientele, and that you could benefit from both the experience and the feedback. Most people understand that starting a business isn't easy, and that everyone needs to start somewhere. If you feel uncomfortable making the offer, choose people who are close to you and who don't mind that you'll be in their personal space for a few hours.

When you perform the service for a friend or relative, treat the job as if it were for a paying client. Ask for feedback on the assignment. Did the service provided meet the assumed client's needs and expectations? Was the service flawless? Consider practice cleaning not only as helpful lessons in learning to accept constructive criticism and feedback, but also as practice in learning to establish ETTs (estimated time on tasks). Which rooms did you feel that you may have spent too much time in, and in which areas could you have spent more time? Be sure to ask these "clients" for permission to use them as references!

Volunteer to Clean for a Nonprofit Organization

This is another wonderful way to gain experience and references, and it will benefit the community at the same time. Check with any organizations that you already belong to and see if they'll let you volunteer a few hours of your time to clean an office, dining hall, lobby, or conference room. Here are some organizations you might want to contact about donating cleaning services:

- a church, temple, or other place of worship
- the Salvation Army or any local shelter or social-service-based program
- schools

- social groups and lodges (for example, the Masonic Temple or the Girl Scouts)
- libraries
- thrift stores

You can also do some research to find community groups that are planning fund-raising events such as flea markets or silent auctions for charity. People donate items such as furniture, books, and toys to be sold at such events, and many local business donate services, which go to the highest bidder. Consider donating a coupon for a free housecleaning. The winning bidder could become a longtime client, and might eventually refer you to others.

Getting started isn't as complicated as you might think. It *is* time consuming, and the research can be frustrating, but you already know that if you want to launch your business with as few problems as possible, you'll have to work at it. Remember that you are building a business, and you'll be working harder for yourself than you ever did for anyone else. So take no shortcuts, and you'll have few surprises.

> **Melinda's Story**
>
> I volunteered to clean offices at my church, which was the meeting place for several support groups on weekday evenings. I committed myself to cleaning the kitchen area twice a week for three weeks. The support groups usually had coffee and pastries, and it was my responsibility to clear the meeting room of plates and coffee cups as well as to clean the kitchen facilities. This experience was so rewarding that I continued to do it for six months. The support groups and the church members were able to benefit from my service: They didn't have to pay someone to do the cleaning, nor did group facilitators have to ask a member to stay behind and clean. I was able to reap a tremendous benefit by being able to use the church as one of my references. It was a great way to start my client base!

How to Get a Business Logo

Early on in the life of your business, although not necessarily before start-up, you'll want a logo. A business logo identifies your company. Think of a few well-known and popular company logos—the Morton's salt girl, AOL's blue triangle, the Nike swoosh—and of how consumers have come to acquaint such logos with a history of quality products and services.

Your logo will also come to reflect your business's positive history. Designing a logo can be tough, though, especially if you aren't artistically inclined. If you can draw a pretty good stick figure but are otherwise hopeless, you'll need outside help.

If you were to hire a graphic arts company to design your logo, you would be looking at a bill of several hundred to several thousand dollars. You must pay for the graphic designer's time—either hourly or as a flat fee per assignment—as well as for the production service: ink, computer software, plates, and so forth. A designer will usually draft three samples. If you don't like any of the three, then you'll pay an extra charge for the next set of samples. Remember that the fees do not include printing services. The designer will deliver a completed logo on a computer disk or CD-ROM; it's your responsibility to find an affordable printer for business cards, brochures, and letterhead.

But there are other sources. One simple solution is to check with your friends and family members. Going with someone you know is often your best bet, because the person already has an idea of the sorts of things you like.

Even if the artist is a friend or family member, don't expect the service or final product to be free. Artists are professionals just like you, and are entitled to receive payment for services rendered. Offer to pay for the service, or suggest that you barter your service for theirs. (Please note, by the way, that the IRS treats barter income just like regular income: You must declare the value of the product or service you receive on your taxes.)

If you can't identify any sources, you can extend your search into the on-line freelance community. Freelancers—also known as consultants, outsourcers, and free agents—are artists who offer their services on a per-assignment basis. There are several on-line sources of freelance artists. Here are a few that have been around for quite a while and have positive feedback within the on-line community:

- Freelance.com
- Freelancers.com
- Elance.com
- DoAProject.com
- FreelanceWorkExchange.com
- WorkExchange.com

Each on-line community works slightly differently, but here's a rough summary of what you can expect:

- You post a job description that details what you want, when you need the work to be completed, and how much you're willing to pay. You might be charged a small fee to post the ad, usually around $25.
- If an artist is interested in your job, she or he will e-mail you for more information and also provide samples of work for you (either at a Web site or as e-mail attachments). Some of the on-line communities include on-line portfolios as part of each artist's profile.
- If you like the work of a particular artist and find that you can work with her or him, you enter into a contract. Either you or the artist can draw up a simple one-page contract that can be e-mailed, signed, and copies scanned or faxed. The contract is between you and the artist, not the sponsor of the freelance database.
- In most cases you'll pay a deposit fee. Most of the owners of on-line databases offer an escrow service: They will hold on to all funds and disburse them upon completion. If the artist is new to the community, or if you're nervous about paying someone who might disappear before your project is delivered, by all means use the escrow service. The cost is minimal, usually a flat fee of $10 to $25. This also protects the artist in case you back out of the contract.
- Pay by credit card whenever possible. Doing so gives you recourse if you experience problems with the artist. Most freelancers are linked with one of the many on-line credit card processing companies, so it's easy to send and receive credit card orders.

Melinda's Story

When I first started my business, there was no way that I could afford to pay more than a few hundred dollars for a professional logo, yet I managed to get my logo for free. One of my clients was a graphic artist for a computer firm. I asked him if he could suggest an affordable designer. He offered his own services for a very reduced fee, then I asked if he'd care to barter his designing services for my housecleaning. He couldn't say yes fast enough. He charged me about $200, and I gave him credit for four housecleaning visits. Simply put, he would have paid me for my service, and I'd have paid him for his, so there was no loss whatsoever. I received a beautiful logo customized just for me. I still use it today.

The Victorian Housecleaner

If you think cleaning today is rough, imagine what life as a housecleaner was like during the Victorian era. There were no vacuum cleaners, washing machines, or indoor plumbing, and there was no such thing as central heat. You had to warm your home with coal-burning stoves, which filled the air with smoke, smut, and ash. The soot from the coal soiled the furniture, draperies, floor, walls, and ceilings. If the soot wasn't cleaned daily, it permanently stained surfaces; even worse, if allowed to linger, it became a dangerous respiratory irritant. The removal of soot and ash was backbreaking work. Only affluent families could afford a housemaid to come into the home to keep on top of the cleaning chores. In fact, a family's social status was determined by the ability to employ servants. Multiple servants were a sign of wealth. Domestic service was a widespread vocational choice; actually, it was the only employment legal for women.

- The artist will send you renditions of the logo in stages. You must approve each change and rendition in writing. When the end product is completed and you approve it, you forward the fee minus the deposit; the project is forwarded to you. It's your responsibility to pay for shipping, handling, and insurance of the logo.

If you're fortunate enough to live in a city with an art school or art institute, consider posting an ad on the school's bulletin board. Give the school a call and find out which department approves such postings; usually it's the office of the registrar or job referral center. You can put all of your information onto a 5-by-7-inch index card, or submit a flyer for posting approval. The school will keep a copy of the posting on file. This protects you and the school if someone were to alter the advertisement—say, changing your dollar figure of $150 to $1,500.

Using a student as the designer of your logo can be beneficial to both of you. You'll be able to get a quality piece of art at a reasonable price, and the student will benefit from the income as well as being able to build her or his portfolio of designs. Student designers may ask to use your logo as a class project that will be submitted for a grade. If the student asks for your written permission, by all means agree to it.

When it comes to the logo itself, keep the design as simple as possible. The least expensive design is black on white, either a pen-and-ink design or a computer-generated model. Black on white easily reproduces in newspapers, on-line, and on business cards and brochures. Logos with color are visually appealing and make wonderful choices, but keep in mind that when you use color it will cost you more in professional printing fees. Even if you choose to print business cards, brochures, and letterhead from your own computer, the color ink cartridge will need to be replaced frequently, and this is expensive.

If money is tight as you start up your business, don't worry about waiting a few months before pursuing a logo. You want the most professional piece of art you can get, so wait until you can afford to spring for it. Don't cut corners and resort to using the copyright-free clip art available on the Web and in stores. Anyone can use clip art—the images are a dime a dozen. Don't sell yourself short when it comes to creating a unique image for your business!

Chapter Four

How to Plan and Develop a Service Manual

O f all business documents, the service manual is the most important. A fully developed service manual explains your service in black and white. A professionally planned and constructed manual will

- separate you from unprofessional and fly-by-night providers,
- fully explain the services that you provide as well as those you *don't,*
- answer frequently asked questions, detail rates, charges, and billing policies, and
- list all contact information for your business.

Most initial contacts will come as a response to your Web site or a newspaper advertisement. Thus your Web page or ad should say, "Call or e-mail for a Guide to Services." Guide to services, service manual, service contract—choose whichever title works for you, but in any case the document will serve as a selling tool and a general handbook for your business. The following pages describe each section of a typical service manual. You can of course make whatever changes you need to suit your individual needs and policies. A sample manual is included at the end of this chapter.

Presentation

Present the manual in an attractive three-ring binder. If you have used color in your company logo, try to find color-coordinated binders. You can also use colored paper that complements the colors of your logo and binder. A visually pleasing presentation will set you apart from other cleaners who give clients poorly typed, handwritten, or photocopied service policies, as well as from those who present nothing at all.

Cover Page

The cover page is the first visual representation of your business that a client sees. It shouldn't be cluttered with information, slogans, or artwork. Keep it simple. Put your logo on the cover page, along with the business name, spelled out in a large, bold font. The information should catch the eye at first glance. Don't forget to include the obvious text: GUIDE TO SERVICES or SERVICE MANUAL. You want to be sure that people know what it is they're reading. Below the title, include:

- the full business name
- your Web address
- the telephone number with area code
- an e-mail address
- the business's mailing address
- a one-line statement of appeal

The statement appeal should be a simple phrase, such as *Serving Chicago since 2001* or *Serving the community of Bridgeport*. Simply said, the statement adds a friendly air to the cover. It should never be gimmicky or contain a sales pitch.

Mission Statement

Every business needs a mission statement. Whether you're selling cars, practicing law, or cleaning homes, the general public deserves to have some idea of why you're in business. Mission statements can be difficult to develop. On the one hand, it's tempting to include the standard buzzwords and phrases, but on the other, such statements are overdone, lack personality, and say nothing about your business.

Take a look at the mission statements of businesses in your area, whether they're one-person operations or multimillion-dollar corporations. Review a dozen or so to see which ones seem professional to you, and which are hokey.

Avoid the standard clichés; clients have seen them all before. Put yourself in the client's place. If you were seeking a housecleaner, would you trust someone whose mission statement included unimaginative phrases such as *reliable service* or *honest and friendly*? I hope not. Use positive but unique phrasing. Tell potential clients something they didn't already know about your company!

Samples of Terrific Mission Statements

- Manor Cleaning Service understands that the demands of modern careers and lifestyles can sometimes create a gap in housecleaning. We aim to bridge that gap by providing professional housecleaning services.
- The mission of Hourglass Cleaners is to provide long- and short-term housecleaning services within the Bay Area. We're proud of our community commitment to providing affordable and customized housecleaning services.

Helpful Phrasing

Desirable	Undesirable
Commitment	We aim to please
Professional	Experienced
Pleased	Satisfied
Prompt	Reliable
Quality	Great/Top-notch
Goal	Want
Affordable	Cheap

Samples of Poor Mission Statements

- At Starbright Cleaners our number one priority is making customers happy! If you want a sparkling-clean home, give us a call. We guarantee our services 100 percent.
  This lacks personality. How are you going to make them happy? What happens if you

can't make them happy? By guaranteeing services, you'll be cleaning a lot of houses for free.

- You've tried the rest, now try the best! Unlike other cleaning services, we here at Zip-E Clean do it right the first time. You can't beat our prices! We're experienced, and we don't cut corners. Cleaning houses is what we do best!

  This statement inspires negative competition, a sign of a nonprofessional. "You can't beat our prices" isn't much of a sales pitch. People should be inspired to call upon you because you're committed to doing what you do, not because you're willing to do it cheaper than the competition.

The Consultation

In most cases you'll be giving a copy of your service manual to prospective clients prior to meeting or speaking with them in depth. You'll want to let them know what to expect from the consultation. In this section of your service manual, you'll briefly explain what happens at the meeting, how long it usually takes, and what days and times you conduct consultations, as well as any information that the client should have ready.

Clientele

Clients like to see what sort of people you currently provide services for. In this section of the manual, you can list what areas you serve; you might also include an analysis of your customer base (even if that's only one client). Perhaps households with two or more children comprise 100 percent of your clientele (if you did only one sample cleaning for someone with two or more children, you're entitled to use that figure). Or maybe 50 percent of your clients are one-person households, or people away from the house more than forty hours per week.

Services

This is the heftiest portion of the manual; it might run upward of twenty pages, or you can reduce it to about five. It all depends on how specific you want to be. We recommend that you be as specific as possible. Somewhere down the line, questions will arise on any issue you haven't considered in your manual.

You can start with a few paragraphs that describe the sort of services you offer, and perhaps one paragraph or a short list of services that you do not provide. Be sure to include:

- whether or not you'll work with pets or children roaming the home
- how you intend to handle cancellations (the client's or yours)
- inclement weather and variances in appointment times due to traffic
- state and federal laws regarding the handling of chemicals
- who is to provide the tools and cleaning products

Confidentiality and Security

Because you'll be storing clients' house keys, you must tell them how and where you do so. Many new clients will be uncomfortable, at least initially, about someone having a set of keys to their home. Put their minds at ease by describing the sort of safe you use (see chapter 8 for information on safes), and your method of handling keys.

You'll also need to assure clients that you hold their e-mail and residential addresses, telephone numbers, and profiles in complete confidentiality. Once you list your business with a newspaper or on a Web site, you'll likely be contacted by all sorts of companies that want to trade customer information with you. Never share this information with anyone. The last thing clients want is to be bombarded with e-mails and telephone solicitors.

Client Mailing List

Here clients are alerted to your biweekly or monthly newsletter (e-mail or snail-mailed). Point out the importance of the newsletters, which will inform clients of

- dates that you may be out of town or on vacation
- holiday reminders
- discounts and specials
- contests
- anticipated delays: bridge construction, closed roads, and so on
- charity and community involvement

Safety

This will be a brief section in which you state how (or if) you'll handle various safety issues.

- Note how you'll handle strangers asking who you are. Sometimes burglars watch a home looking to identify the specific routines of people coming and going.
- Mention whether you'll work among other service providers (child care provider, roofer, plumber, and the like). Many cleaners opt not to work alongside other providers. Other service people tend to clutter up cleaned rooms, and they can be distracting. Consider also the safety risks: You don't want the baby-sitter to slip on the kitchen floor that you just mopped, for instance. It's fair to decline to work in a home where other people or service providers are present.
- Clients should be told that they need to give you notice if someone will be in the home, either working or visiting. You don't want to walk into a home and scare someone (or yourself) because no one was expecting you.
- Clients need to tell you about of any safety faults in the home. One client neglected to explain that the kitchen's hot- and cold-water faucets were installed incorrectly: The hot water was located on the right rather than the left. You'll need to know of any plumbing problems, broken steps, exposed wiring, and so forth.

When it comes to safety, you can't be too cautious.

Rates

This comes toward the end of the manual. You want people to learn about you and your services before they get to your rates. This is also why the manual does not have a table of contents: Readers will go straight for rates and ignore everything else.

Note in this section whether you charge by the hour or by the assignment. Also, don't forget to mention:

- How long the rates are good for (one year, or subject to change without notice).
- Weekend and holiday rates. If you don't work on New Year's Day, or if you will work but charge time and a half, let clients know.

- Discounts for referrals, monthly plans, or any other promotions that you've developed.

See chapter 3 for a description of how to set rates.

Scheduling

This tells clients how to obtain your services. Some cleaners set up a regular service schedule; some ask clients to confirm each appointment ahead of time. This section of your manual will outline your policy.

- Should regulars (say, once-a-week clients) confirm with you each week? Should clients call two weeks in advance of the intended day? Or should regular clients call only to change or cancel an appointment?
- How can the client reach you—phone, e-mail, beeper, or cell phone?
- Give a cut-off time for reservations (for example, by 8:00 P.M. Friday for the following week) or else you'll be bombarded with last-minute requests!

Cancellations

This will come to be of grave importance to you. There's nothing worse than having a client call and cancel two hours before a scheduled cleaning. You'll need a firm (*very* firm!) policy about how you will handle cancellations.

- You'll need to give clients a time period in which to cancel without penalty (for example, forty-eight hours in advance).
- Will you charge for cancellations with less than forty-eight hours' notice? If so, how much?
- What will happen if you wake up with the flu? Will you reschedule appointments for the following week? What about bimonthly clients—will they have to wait an entire month before services resume?
- Be sure to include a statement such as *Frequent cancellations may result in termination of services.* It gives you something to fall back on should you ever have to terminate a client who cancels services more often than she or he receives them.

Billing and Payments

As a professional service provider, you'll establish a method of billing. In this section, be specific as to when clients can expect their billing statements. Consider:

- Will you be billing on a weekly, biweekly, or monthly basis?
- How will the statements be sent: mailed, left at the residence, or e-mailed?
- What is the grace period between the statement date and the due date?
- What happens if payment is made late or not at all?
- What payment options do you offer (credit cards, checks, money orders)?
- Do you require a deposit from new clients?
- Do you offer bartering services? (This is a great way to give and get needed services!)
- What is the turnaround time for receipts? How and when should the client expect to receive her or his receipt?

I strongly recommend that you refrain from a cash-only policy. It gives an unprofessional impression. Also, as a sole proprietorship you are responsible for your own taxes. Dealing with cash is tricky; it's too easy to put it into your pocket, spend it, and not record it.

Instead, you need to create a paper trail for each transaction. Insist on personal checks or credit cards (see chapter 2 for information on how to accept credit card payments). If clients must pay with cash, never allow them to leave it sitting unattended, such as on a kitchen counter. It's too easy for someone else to come along and take your money, and you have no proof that you didn't receive the cash. Save yourself the headache by insisting on checks and credit cards.

Contract Renewal

Don't forget to mention the dates of validity for the contract—is it good for a year, or six months? Include the date and year of expiration. Add a line or two to inform clients that they will be given ample time to read and review any changes or updates to the contract.

Community and Charitable Causes

Many business proprietors overlook the importance of charitable causes. Donating your services (offering to clean a church twice a year, for example) or sending a $10 check once a month to a community charity goes a long way. Make the contribution in the name of the business (it's tax deductible), and mention the charity here in a list of your contributions. Clients will appreciate the fact that you aren't all about the money.

General Information

Finally, you should include your insurance information: the name of the insurance company, your account number, and a toll-free number for clients to call and verify your coverage. Remember that you'll be handling the client's personal and prized belongings. Don't be insulted if someone does in fact call the insurance company. Also include the name and toll-free telephone number of your bonding company, and your bond certificate number.

It's a nice touch to include coupons for cleaning products. Be sure to check the expiration dates! You might also want to include business cards for other small businesses that offer services your clients may request: pet-sitting, yard tending, child care, power washing, errand services, and so forth. Once your business is established, you can network with many of these businesses for referrals.

Room Plans

At the back of the service manual, include a set of room plans. These are blank forms that you and the client can fill out together during the in-home consultation. They list exactly what tasks are to be performed in each room of the house. This lets the client know what services to expect, and it will help you develop the estimated time on tasks that enable you to set fees and schedules. Blank room plans are included in Appendix III, at the back of this book. You can adapt these forms to fit your own needs.

Guide to Services
Colonial Village Cleaners

www.ColonialVillageCleaners.com

E-mail: Mjones@ColonialVillageCleaners.com

123 Brownstone Street

Cleveland, Ohio 12345

(123) 555–1234

Serving the suburban Cleveland community

Thank you for inquiring about house and apartment cleaning services provided by Colonial Village Cleaners!

Mission Statement

Colonial Village Cleaners is a house- and apartment-cleaning service that provides professional cleaning to suburban Cleveland. The suburban community recognizes us as leaders in home and apartment cleaning. We've been serving the community since November 2000! Our mission is to provide affordable cleaning services so that people will not be overwhelmed with day-to-day household responsibilities.

Initial Contact

Prospective clients may either phone (123) 555–1234 or send an e-mail inquiry to Mjones@ColonialVillageCleaners.com. In return, a copy of the *Guide to Services* will be e-mailed as a Word document, or snail-mailed to an address that you specify. After reading our literature, you are encouraged to phone or e-mail with any questions or concerns. If you choose to hire our services, you should then call or e-mail to schedule a weekend appointment for an in-home consultation. Please note that all consultations are scheduled on either a Saturday or a Sunday.

Sample Service Manual, Page 1

The Consultation

Prospective clients and Mary Jones, the owner and service provider of Colonial Village Cleaners, and if applicable, an owner-assigned independent contractor, will meet at the client's home for a consultation that generally lasts between thirty and sixty minutes.

During the consultation the following items will be discussed:

- We'll review your household needs as well as Colonial Village Cleaners' policies, service guide, payments, schedules, and any questions you might have.
- A sample home-cleaning plan, complete with room-by-room checklists, will be developed and available for your review within two business days. Once reviewed and approved, you and Mary Jones will sign the service contract and arrange a date for services to begin.
- Emergency information forms will be filled out.

A set of keys is to be provided to Mary Jones upon the signing of the service contract. Please note that we do not make secondary or follow-up visits to pick up or drop off keys or to pick up payments. If pickup or drop-off services are requested, you'll be charged the nominal hourly rate of $25 for each visit. You are more than welcome to make an appointment to pick up or drop off keys or payments at 123 Brownstone Street in Cleveland.

Please keep in mind that the consultation is a time for all parties to meet and share information regarding the servicing of the home. Not all cleaner–client matches are appropriate; therefore we reserve the right to decline services.

Clientele

Colonial Village Cleaners provides house- and apartment-cleaning services to residents of suburban Cleveland. Approximately 70 percent of our client base consists of one-person households in which the resident works away from home an average of twelve hours per day, or sixty hours per week. The remaining 30 percent of our clients are families with multiple responsibilities: children, family activities, and involvement with community events.

Sample Service Manual, Page 2

Our Services

Visits are between two and four hours long, depending on the needs of your household.

Colonial Village Cleaners will:

- Give you a set time for your cleaning, with a one-hour variance to allow for traffic and road conditions.
- Complete all services described in the home plan, and leave a completed plan on the dining room table or other designated area.
- Use products that you choose and purchase; please have adequate supplies replenished on a weekly basis.
- Make suggestions with regard to cleaning products and procedures to ensure prompt and thorough cleaning of the household.
- Dispose of chemicals in a utility or other sink that you designate.
- Bring in mail and newspapers if asked to do so.
- Put out or bring in residential trash cans if our visit coincides with your trash pickup day and time.
- Send a monthly newsletter via e-mail (blind carbon copy) to inform clients of news, vacation dates, contests, and so forth.
- Maintain client house keys, home plans, and alarm codes in a fireproof safe at the residence of Mary Jones, proprietor.

Colonial Village Cleaners does not:

- Provide service during the summer months to homes without adequate air-conditioning.
- Provide service during the winter months to homes without adequate heating.
- Provide service to households with unsupervised pets (please gate or crate your pet).
- Provide service to households during the times that the house is occupied by unsupervised children or teenagers.
- Provide services other than housecleaning; please feel free to inquire about referrals for vendors of other services.

Sample Service Manual, Page 3

- Operate washing machines, dryers, stoves, trash compactors, or other electric, gas, or kerosene appliances.
- Operate your motor vehicle.
- Throw circuit breakers or replace fuses.
- Let in service people such as water meter readers, UPS drivers, and so forth.
- Feed pets or clean up pet accidents.

We also do not:
- Access your phone or answering machine.
- Exchange keys with anyone other than the contracted client.
- Use any chemical cleaning product not specified in writing.
- Sell or share residential or e-mail addresses, names, or telephone numbers with any other company or organization.

Hours of Operation

Colonial Village Cleaners generally provides services between 7:00 A.M. and 6:00 P.M. Business hours for voice mail are between 9:00 A.M. and 8:00 P.M.; e-mail may be sent at any time. When phoning or e-mailing reservations, always wait for a confirmation. Our general response time is forty-eight hours.

Inclement Weather

Colonial Village Cleaners will provide limited, delayed, or no service during incidents of inclement weather:
- We will not provide mobile service during snow, sleet, ice, or hurricane-like weather. The only clients we service during extreme weather conditions are those within a safe walking distance from the residence of Mary Jones or the assigned independent contractor.
- Limited or delayed service may occur in extreme thunderstorms, in dangerously cold or hot conditions, and in any city- or state-declared weather emergency.
- All visits during a period of inclement weather will be on an hourly advisory status depending on the driving conditions.

Sample Service Manual, Page 4

Safety

Colonial Village Cleaners asks you to inform trustworthy neighbors, neighborhood watch organizations, relatives, and so forth that a housecleaner will be on your property. Doing so can save the police department, neighbors, and the housecleaner from an embarrassing situation.

Please notify Colonial Village Cleaners in advance (a few days is ideal) of any person or people who may be in your home during the time of the housecleaning service. This includes family members, service contractors, repair personnel, and so forth. Colonial Village Cleaners reserves the right to reschedule visits that coincide with a visit by another service contractor or houseguest.

Rates

- Initial consultations are free of charge.
- Each two-hour weekday visit to an apartment or house is $50.
- Each four-hour weekday visit to an apartment or house is $80.
- Each additional weekday hour beyond a four-hour visit is $22.
- Weekend visits are billed at the rate of $75 per two-hour visit.
- Colonial Village Cleaners offers a 10 percent discount to senior citizens and college students.

Reservations

To schedule a weekly visit, please phone or e-mail your reservation by 10:00 P.M. Friday for the following week. Please note that we do not use cell phones or beepers within the company. Always wait for a confirmation via e-mail or telephone.

We can sometimes accommodate unplanned requests if we have a cancellation. However, we can rarely do so with less than twenty-four hours' notice.

Cancellations

- Please phone or e-mail (and wait for a confirmation) for all cancellations.
- Cancellations with less than forty-eight hours' notice (weekends and holidays included) are charged the nominal two-hour rate of $50. The only exception is inclement weather.

Sample Service Manual, Page 5

- Excessive cancellations with less than forty-eight hours' notice are subject to cessation of services.

Please be sure of all dates and times when you e-mail or phone in your request. Calling to cancel on the morning of a scheduled visit or two hours prior to the visit is inappropriate. We understand that emergencies arise, and that you may need to occasionally cancel services with less than forty-eight hours' notice. However, please reserve such cancellations for emergencies only.

Billing and Payments

A billing statement will be prepared every Monday and either e-mailed to you or left at your residence. Payment is expected within four days (weekends and holidays included).

Payment Options
- You may leave a check or money order at your residence on the day of the service. Please make all checks and money orders payable to Colonial Village Cleaners.
- Please do not postdate checks or money orders.
- You may mail a check or money order. Note that payments received after the due date are subject to late fees.
- You may pay with Visa, MasterCard, American Express, or Discover Card. We accept credit card payments through PayPal.com. Please ask for information on how to set up a free account with PayPal. PayPal is secure and encrypted.
- For security reasons, we do not accept cash left at residences. If you would like to pay in cash, please call or e-mail Mary Jones to arrange a drop-off time at 123 Brownstone Street.
- Occasionally we barter for services. If you've a professional service that you think may be of use to us, please feel free to ask! We've bartered services for graphic arts, pet-sitting, landscaping, and more. Bartering is one way that communities and small businesses can help each other.

Sample Service Manual, Page 6

Colonial Village Cleaners will issue a receipt within forty-eight hours after the payment is received. The receipt will be sent to you via e-mail or left at your residence. In some cases, a receipt may be snail-mailed to an address specified by the client.

Late Payments

Payments that are received beyond the due date listed on your billing statement are subject to late fees of $1.00 a day (weekends and holidays included) until the account is brought up to date.

In cases of frequent late payments, Colonial Village Cleaners reserves the right to terminate services.

Additional fees may be imposed for returned checks and closed accounts. In such cases, you will be charged $30 for each returned check (that's the service fee imposed on us by our bank), and any additional bank fees that are charged to us, as well as daily late fees that accrue until the account is brought up to date.

Referrals

Colonial Village Cleaners offers a 50 percent discount on any one (1) four-hour visit for all completed referrals. This is our way of saying thanks to our wonderful and committed clients!

Below are two people who have given permission to be contacted for assignment-based references:

John Brown
123 Center Street
Cleveland, Ohio 12345
(123) 555–4444

Jane Doe
123 Round Street
Cleveland, Ohio 12345
(123) 555–2121

Contracts

Colonial Village Cleaners updates service guides and contracts on January 1 of each year. You will always receive a copy of the new contract in the month of December. This gives you an opportunity to read and review the guide as well as to ask questions.

Sample Service Manual, Page 7

How to Plan and Develop a Service Manual

Community and Education

Colonial Village Cleaners provides some services free of charge to terminally ill Cleveland residents. Please ask for further information. We honor our commitment to helping community members in their time of need.

Colonial Village Cleaners is a member of the Cleveland Citizens Drug Awareness Program, and is represented by Mary Jones, proprietor. We donate annually to the organization's fund to send disadvantaged children to summer camp. Mary Jones also sponsors and mentors a young person currently enrolled in the program.

General Information

Colonial Village Cleaners is insured and bonded by:

Generations Insurance Company of Ohio
P.O. Box 1234
Akron, Ohio 12345
(888) 555–5555
Account Number: 123-456-789

Colonial Village Cleaners is also bonded by:

Generations Insurance Company of Ohio
P.O. Box 5678
Akron, Ohio 12345
(888) 555–1111
Certificate Number: 789456

Colonial Village Cleaners is licensed as a service provider by the city of Cleveland. A copy of our business license is attached.

Home Plan

A home plan is a step-by-step guide for cleaning your home. We will review each room that you have requested to be cleaned, listing all required cleaning tasks for that room

Sample Service Manual, Page 8

and which products will be used. We also include an estimated task time (ETT). This will give all parties an idea of the total amount of time necessary to complete a house-cleaning.

Estimated task times take into consideration:

- Cleaning behind heavy objects or several small objects that may need to be moved. An example might be removing a collection of glass jars from a table-top, cleaning the jars as well as the tabletop, and returning the jars to the table-top.
- Thorough indoor window cleaning: inside double-hung panes, as well the in-ward pane.
- Any buildup of kitchen grease, pet hair, hard water and lime stains, or wax residue.
- Intricate objects such as glass figurines or books that need to be removed, cleaned, and replaced.

Please understand that a thorough cleaning is a time-consuming process. We give added care and take precautions with furniture, collectibles, and other objects.

If you wish to make a change to the home plan after it has been completed and signed, please alert Mary Jones in writing, and allow two full weeks for a second draft to be drawn, reviewed, and signed, and for a copy to be provided to you. Remember that making changes to a home plan means that the ETT will change. This may decrease or increase the time allotment necessary for service provision. We thus encourage you to carefully review your initial home plan.

After the home plan has been accepted, please do not ask us to perform tasks that are not part of the contract. We will only provide the services included on the home plan.

Sample Service Manual, Page 9

Home Plan for John Burns, 456 Green Street

Client _____   Home telephone _____

E-mail address _____   Work telephone _____

Pets _____   Cell phone _____

Home alarm system _____ yes _____ no

Home alarm system code and instructions _____

Telephone number of home alarm system provider _____

Dates valid: _____ through _____

Emergency Information

Telephone number of contractor or repair person _____

Cell phone number of contractor or repair person _____

Alternate Key Holders

Name _____   Name _____

Address _____   Address _____

Telephone _____   Telephone _____

Cell phone _____   Cell phone _____

Relationship to client _____   Relationship to client _____

Telephone and Account Numbers (where applicable)

Gas company _____

Electric company _____

Water bureau _____

Telephone company _____

Fire department _____

Police department _____

Poison control _____

Sample Room Plans, Page 1

Client: John Burns   **Room: Vestibule**

Floor Finish

Wood ___X___ Carpet _____ Tile _____

Other _____

1. Dry-mop.
2. Apply one coat of Albert's Wood Floor Cleaner.

Wall Finish

Wood paneling _____ Tile _____ Paint over plaster _____

Washable wallpaper over plaster _____ Wood wainscoting ___X___

Plastic wainscoting _____ Other _____

1. Swipe with electrostatic dry wipe.
2. Wipe down handprints and smudges with Fantastik brand cleaner.

Entrance Door

Wood _____ Metal ___X___

Door windows ___X___

1. Metal door to be sprayed and wiped with Fantastik brand cleaner.
2. Door windows to be spayed with CleanBrite glass cleaner and wiped with a lint-free paper towel.
3. Inside and outside doorknobs to be wiped with a lint-free paper towel. No cleaning solvents to be used on the antique metal doorknobs or outside door knocker.

ETT: 20 Minutes (Vestibule)

Sample Room Plans, Page 2

Client: John Burns   **Room: Living Room**

Floor Finish

Wood _____ Carpet ___X___ Tile _____

Other _____

1. Vacuum with Carpet Fresh.

Wall Finish

Wood paneling _____ Tile _____ Paint over plaster ___X___

Washable wallpaper over plaster _____ Wood wainscoting __X__

Plastic wainscoting _____ Other _____

1. Swipe with electrostatic dry wipe.
2. Handprints and smudges on wood wainscoting to be wiped down with Murphy's brand wood cleaner.
3. Painted wall surface to be wiped with an electrostatic lint-free cloth.
4. Wooden crevices can be blotted with a paper towel and vinegar diluted with two parts water.

Appliances

Televison ___X___ VCR _____ Stereo component unit___X___ Humidifier ___X___

Other _____

1. Television and stereo to be wiped down with Fantastik brand cleaner and dry-wiped with electrostatic lint-free cloth.
2. Humidifier to be cleaned externally with CleanBrite brand glass cleaner.

Other Furnishings

Coffee table ___X___ Bookcase___4___ End table ___2___ Paintings ___2___

Sample Room Plans, Page 3

Metal and glass lamp fixtures ___2 (1 standing and 1 tabletop)_____

Miscellaneous _____

1. Two oil paintings on the wall to be lightly feather-dusted.
2. Books to be removed from bookcases and wiped with paper towel. Bookcase to be wiped down with Pledge anti-dust formula.
3. Metal lamp fixtures to be swiped with feather duster and glass portions wiped with CleanBrite glass cleaner.
4. Coffee table and end tables to be polished with Pledge anti-dust formula.

ETT: 30 Minutes (Living Room)

Sample Room Plans, Page 4

Client: John Burns   **Room: Kitchen**

Floor Finish

Wood _____ Linoleum ___X__ Tile _____

Other _____

1. Dry-mop.
2. Clean with Lysol kitchen cleaner.

Wall Finish

Wood paneling _____ Tile _____ Paint over plaster ___X__

Washable wallpaper over plaster ___X__ Wood wainscoting _____

Plastic wainscoting _____

Other _____

1. Swipe painted wall surface with electrostatic dry wipe.
2. Wipe down wallpapered surface with damp paper towel.

Countertop

Wood _____ Fiberglass _____ Tile ___X__

Other _____

1. Kitchen countertop to be wiped down with Lysol brand tile cleaner and a damp sponge (*note that grout is permanently stained).

Sink

Porcelain ___X__ Acrylic _____ Stainless steel _____

Other _____

1. Kitchen sink to be washed with Lysol brand kitchen cleaner and a damp sponge—no abrasives (*note that the kitchen's porcelain surface is scratched and permanently stained).

Sample Room Plans, Page 5

2. Chrome fixtures to be cleaned with CleanBrite glass cleaner and a damp sponge, and dried with a paper towel.

Appliances

Stove __X__ Garbage disposal _____ Dishwasher _____
Refrigerator __X__ Trash compactor _____ Microwave oven __X__
Toaster oven __X__ Other _____

1. External surface of stove to be wiped with Lysol brand kitchen cleaner (*note that around the burners is a heavy buildup of cooking deposits that cannot be removed by the housecleaner).
2. External surface of refrigerator to be wiped with Fantastik brand cleaner.
3. Microwave oven to be cleaned externally and internally with Henkel's brand microwave cleaner and damp sponge.
4. Toaster oven to be emptied of crumbs and cleaned externally with Henkel's brand microwave cleaner and damp sponge.

Miscellaneous Tasks

1. Plastic kitchen trash can to be soaked in Lysol, rinsed, and wiped dry with paper towel.
2. Kitchen trash to be placed in trash bin outdoors.
3. Collection of ceramic cookie jars to be cleaned with Fantastik brand cleaner.
4. Wooden cabinets to be wiped with OrangeSol degreaser formula and damp sponge.
5. Small kitchen window to be cleaned (inside only) with CleanBrite glass cleaner and paper towels.

ETT: 30 Minutes (Kitchen)

Sample Room Plans, Page 6

Client: John Burns   **Room: Bathroom**

Floor

Laminate ___X___ Tile _____ Marble _____

Other _____

1. Floor to be dry-mopped and wet-mopped with Pergo brand floor cleaner (sprayed on and mopped with damp sponge mop).

Tub/Shower

Fiberglass ___X___ Porcelain _____ Ceramic tile _____

Other _____chrome fixtures_____

1. Tub and shower unit to be cleaned with Bon Ami brand cleaner and rinsed clean.
2. Chrome fixtures to be cleaned with Henderson's premoistened chrome cleaning wipes.

Toilet

1. Toilet bowl to be cleaned with Lysol brand toilet cleaner and brush.
2. Toilet surfaces to be cleaned with Formula 409 brand cleaner and wiped with lint-free soft cloth.

Walls

Wooden wainscoting ___X___ Painted plaster ___X___ Tile _____

Other _____

1. Wooden wainscoting to be wiped free of smudges and fingerprints with Fantastik brand cleaner and a damp paper towel.
2. Painted plaster walls to be wiped with OrangeSol brand cleaner and damp lint-free paper towel.

Sample Room Plans, Page 7

Vanity

Porcelain ___X___ Stainless steel _____ Acrylic _____ Formica _____

Wood _____ Glass _____ Chrome ___X___

Other _____

1. Formica vanity to be wiped with Fantastik brand cleaner and lint-free soft cloth.
2. Porcelain sink to be cleaned with Formula 409 brand cleaner and wiped with lint-free soft cloth.
3. Chrome fixtures to be cleaned with Henderson's premoistened chrome cleaning wipes.
4. Mirror above vanity to be cleaned with CleanBrite glass cleaner and lint-free paper towels.
5. Glass vases on vanity to be wiped with an electrostatic cloth.

Door

Wood ___X___ Glass ___X___ Other _____

1. Wooden door to be dusted with feather duster, then damp-wiped with Murphy's brand wood cleaner and damp sponge.
2. Glass mirror on door's inside to be cleaned with CleanBrite glass cleaner and lint-free paper towel.

Towel Rack and Wall Decorations

Chrome _____ Wood ___X___ Acrylic _____ Glass ___X___

Other _____

1. Wooden towel rack to be cleaned with electrostatic cloth.
2. Three wooden picture frames to be cleaned with electrostatic cloth.
3. Glass on picture frames to be cleaned with CleanBrite brand glass cleaner and lint-free paper towel.

ETT: 30 Minutes (Bathroom)

Sample Room Plans, Page 8

Client: John Burns   **Room: Bedroom 1**

Floor

Carpet ___X___ Wood ___X___ Tile _____

Other _____

1. Carpet to be vacuumed with Carpet Fresh.
2. Wood portions to be dry-mopped then lightly mopped with Pledge spray-on floor cleaner and damp sponge mop.

Nightstand and Dresser

Wood ___X___ Glass_____ Acrylic ___X___

Other _____

1. Wooden nightstand to be cleaned with Pledge brand wood cleaner and lint-free paper towel.
2. Dresser to be cleaned with Pledge brand wood cleaner after decorative acrylic items are removed.
3. Decorative acrylic boxes to be cleaned with Fantastik brand cleaner and lint-free soft cloth.

ETT: 30 Minutes (Bedroom 1)

Sample Room Plans, Page 9

Client: John Burns   **Room: Laundry Room**

Metal Appliances

Washer___X___ Dryer___X___

1. Washer and dryer to be cleaned with Fantastik brand cleaner.

Utility Sink

Acrylic ___X___ Stainless steel _____ Other _____

1. Acrylic utility sink to be cleaned out with Pine-Sol brand cleaner and wiped with paper towels.

ETT: 10 minutes (Laundry Room)

Sample Room Plans, Page 10

How to Plan and Develop a Service Manual

Home Plan: John Burns, 456 Green Street

Vestibule:	20 minutes
Living Room:	30 minutes
Kitchen:	30 minutes
Bathroom:	30 minutes
Bedroom 1:	30 minutes
Laundry Room:	10 minutes
Total time:	2 hours 30 minutes

Charge: $70

I have read the service guide and agree to the home plan that has been supplied to me by Mary Jones of Colonial Village Cleaners. I agree to the policies as described in the manual, as well as to the customized home plan that has been developed for me.

_____   _____

(Client Signature)   (Date)

_____   _____

Mary Jones, Colonial Village Cleaners   (Date)

Sample Room Plans, Page 11

Chapter Five

How to Screen Clients

Not all cleaner–client matches are ideal. That's why screening your clients is so important. If you do a careful job of screening and keep an eye out for potential problems, you and your clients will both be happy.

By Telephone

The phone rings—and there's a potential client on the other end! It's human nature to stutter and forget your memorized speech. It's good to remember that almost no one notices nervousness. It will also help if you write your greeting spiel down on an index card that you keep by the telephone. If you get nervous, you can refer to it.

The first question a client usually asks is "What are your rates?" Head off this question by asking if she or he has received your *Guide to Services*. Take a few minutes to explain your policy of sending this guide to the client for review, and that the next step is to schedule an in-home consultation. Never quote prices or give estimates over the telephone, no matter how insistent the caller is. You have more to offer than just a price, and you want to make sure callers understand everything your business can do for them.

You should also use this time to ask the client where she or he lives. If it's an area that's not in your zone, you've already saved yourself time and trouble. Be sure to refer the caller to a cleaner who does service the area.

If the caller has already received the *Guide to Services* and is phoning to schedule a consultation, congratulations! This means that the client has read the information, finds it acceptable, and is ready to meet you. Ask if you can answer any questions, and reiterate that the purpose of the consultation is to produce an initial home plan. When making arrangements for an in-home consultation, be sure to get detailed directions to the client's home. Regardless of the directions the client gives, check out a city map, or go to one of the free on-line map services such as Mapquest.com and download a copy of the directions. Having a map will allow you to choose an alternate route in case of unexpected road construction or detours.

Be safety conscious when agreeing to meet a stranger. Tell a family member or a friend where you're going and when you expect to return. If anything sounds suspicious about the caller, mention that you'll be bringing a companion. Inviting friends along on in-home consultations isn't very professional, however, so if you're not sure about the integrity of the caller, it's better not to take a chance. Sometimes callers sound strange because they're uncomfortable talking on the phone, or they aren't sure what to say or ask. Use your best judgment. If something doesn't seem quite right, it probably isn't.

Don't forget to ask the client about household pets. It would not serve you well to be greeted at the front door by a German shepherd if you're afraid of or allergic to dogs.

Ask the client where she or he heard about your services: Web site, business card, or referral? This is great feedback for your marketing strategy. If you printed 200 flyers, tacked them to bulletin boards, and left them at various establishments—and none of your callers mentions the flyer—then you've learned how not to advertise.

In Person

Carry a service bag that will hold extra copies of your *Guide to Services*, information forms, business cards, and blank room plans, as well as a map, clipboard, notebook, small stapler, pens, and pencils. Keep everything labeled and organized so you don't have to fumble.

When you greet the client, be sure to give a firm handshake. This shows confidence and respect. Explain to the client that the consultation process generally takes an hour, or whatever time limit you've specified in your manual.

Ask the client to give you a tour of the home. For each room that you're shown, take a room plan sheet and fill out the header to indicate the room. It should take fifteen minutes or so to do an initial tour. Don't worry about writing down anything yet; you'll be doing a second walk-through.

When the initial tour is completed, you and the client will go through each room a second time. During the second walk-through, the client identifies the specific services requested. Use this time to clarify services and requests as well as the products to be used. Here are some things to keep in mind:

- **Point out and ask about furniture or fixtures that the client didn't specify.** During the second walk-through, for instance, you might notice a mirror behind the bathroom door that the client didn't mention. Is this to be cleaned as well?
- **Ask about the handling of fragile or decorative items.** Use your judgment with fragile items. If you don't feel comfortable being asked to clean an original Tiffany lamp, say so!
- **Ask about household pets.** If there's a dog, where will it be while you're working in the home? Are there any exotic family pets that you need to know about—say, 50-foot boa constrictors caged in the basement, or a tarantula kept under a teenager's bed?
- **Ask who will be in the home when you are cleaning: unsupervised children, a grandmother, another service provider?** Be cautious here. You don't want to sound suspicious of the client's household members, but you are entitled to work in peace and comfort, without feeling as though someone's watching you. You dictate what's comfortable for you.
- **Avoid making any sort of commitment to the assignment, dates, or times.** Review with the client how the estimate process works. You'll take the written information and draw up an estimate that includes a total ETT, rate, and schedule of availability. The client will receive a copy and will have a few days to verify the estimate. Inevitably, a client will have forgotten a task, or will want to remove one. This means that you need to reevaluate the home plan. It may take a week or so before you can negotiate a complete home plan. Still, it's better to take the extra week now than to get halfway through a daily assignment only to have the client add or remove a task.
- **You are interviewing the client as much as the client is interviewing you.** If anything about the client or the home makes you feel uncomfortable, speed up the consultation process, thank the client, say you'll be in touch, and get out. Wait a

few days and instead of submitting an estimate, send a note apologizing for not realizing how swamped you really are—or something to that effect. You're going to meet all kinds of people and see all kinds of homes. Some are not desirable, and it's best to politely refuse these assignments from the start rather than having to bail out later.

Sooner or later, you'll be called to give an estimate on a home that is in an unsanitary and deplorable condition. It's uncomfortable, to say the least. You should smile, however, and treat the client with respect; that evening write an apologetic note and refuse the assignment. You might choose to tell the truth about why you are refusing, but if you're uncomfortable with that, then a white lie is perfectly fine.

Once you've left the client's home, be sure to follow through with providing the estimate by the stated date. If your estimate is late, you're sending the message that you have difficulties with promptness, and that's not a great first impression. If you don't hear from the client within a day or two of dropping off the estimate, give a call. If changes need to be made, do so immediately, and get the corrected copy to the client within two business days of the requested change.

If the prospective client agrees to the services you've outlined, celebrate—but also think about committing yourself to two cleanings only; at that point, you and the client can both have a chance to reevaluate things and make sure the match is right. This gives you an easy way out of a contract if anything about the assignment turns out to make you uncomfortable. (See chapter 13 for more.)

Now it's time to roll up your sleeves and go to work!

The Victorian Butler

In the late nineteenth century, a butler's duties ranged from maintaining and accounting for the household's china, silver, glassware, and linens to answering the door for callers. The butler also held the keys to the wine cellar, where his responsibilities included decanting wines and choosing the correct vintage to complement each meal. Depending on the household, the butler was also known to brew beer. He assisted at meals by pouring coffee or tea for breakfast and by pouring wine for dinner. During the meals, when he wasn't pouring, the butler stood behind the master's chair.

Chapter Six
Cleaning 101

Yes, you've cleaned before. But do you know how to clean in the most efficient, stress-free way possible? How to shop for supplies and take care of your aching back? As you embark on your new career, you'll quickly develop cleaning methods that work for you. Here are a few tips and tricks to help get you started in the right direction.

The Well-Stocked Cleaner

First of all, you've got a decision to make: Do you want to use your clients' cleaning supplies and equipment, or do you want to bring your own? If you're just starting out and short on cash, using clients' products could be the way to go. It doesn't involve any cash outlay for you, and you don't have to worry about clients not liking your products. In addition, you'll save yourself the aches and pains of lugging products in and out of your clients' homes.

Still, bringing your own supplies has a lot of advantages. These include:

- You can stick with the products that work best for you, saving time and energy when you clean.
- You don't have to worry that your clients will run out of the products you need.
- You can organize your products in a caddy and/or cleaning apron that you bring with you on every job. You'll know exactly where everything is all the time, and you'll save time (and footsteps!) by having it at your side.

- You know exactly how to use each product, and what it's best for.
- Ecologically friendly, hypoallergenic, scent-free, and superstrength products are all available, and offering these to your clients can be a strong selling point for your business.
- You'll simply project a sharper, more businesslike, more professional image.

Of course, if a client prefers a certain product, good customer service dictates that you use it.

There are countless cleaning products on the market, and you'll want to do some experimenting to see what you like. It's easiest to buy your products from a retail outlet: grocery stores, discount houses, and drugstores all stock good brands. Do some comparison shopping, however. Janitorial supply firms and many companies on the Internet offer specialized products that might be much better suited to your needs. You can also find concentrates that allow you to mix your own cleaning solutions in spray bottles; these save money and packaging. The busier you are, the more it's worth taking the time to find products you can really trust.

What does a well-supplied housecleaner need? Here's a list of some essentials that you can start with. Of course, you'll want to tailor it to fit your own and your clients' needs.

- **Cleaning caddy.** This is a fantastic time saver! Make sure it's deep enough to prevent products from tipping over. Look for a comfortable carrying handle too.
- **Cleaning apron.** You can carry many supplies and products right on your person if you have a cleaning apron with lots of pockets and hooks. Cloths, towels, brushes, spray bottles, and more can all be kept here. You can even make or adapt your own cleaning apron for maximum efficiency.
- **Mild all-purpose cleaner** for countertops, faucets, cabinets, and the like. Spray bottles are handiest.
- **Disinfectant cleaner** for bathroom and kitchen cleaning. Again, use a spray bottle.
- **Abrasive cleaner,** but not too abrasive. A mild formulation won't damage surfaces.
- **Glass cleaner** for glass, mirrors, TVs, and shiny black appliances.

Choosing a Vacuum

Investing in a top-notch vacuum cleaner may be one of the wisest moves you can make. Yes, they're expensive: hundreds of dollars for the best quality. And you might not be able to afford one right away. But a good vacuum will save you a lot of time and energy; you'll get the same results (or better) with far less work. The best vacuums allow you to offer clients a level of cleaning they'll never achieve on their own. That's a strong selling point for your services!

When you are ready to make the investment, here are some things to consider as you decide on which vacuum is right for you:

- **Type.** Upright or canister? Uprights work well on wall-to-wall carpeting, but they don't reach under furniture. Canisters work well on all kinds of surfaces, are much more flexible, and are generally a better bet for the housecleaner.
- **Airflow.** Measured in cfm (cubic feet per minute), this is the real indicator of a vacuum's efficiency. It tells you how much suction power the machine has. The higher, the better.
- **Amps.** A high-amp vacuum is not necessarily a stronger one; it just uses more electricity. Airflow is a more important characteristic to look for in judging vacuums.
- **Attachments.** Does the model have the attachments you need? Can you add new attachments later as your needs change?
- **Cost and ease of maintenance.** What will you have to pay for replacement bags, belts, and filters? Are they readily available? What about repairs—are there good repair resources at a convenient distance from you, and are they affordable?
- **Filtration quality.** Some canister-type vacuums can filter out allergenic particles; this might be important to some of your clients. Look for HEPA (high-efficiency particulate air) or ULPA (ultra low penetration air) filters if any of your clients suffer from respiratory or other allergy problems. These vacuums are, of course, more expensive.
- **Comfort.** You'll be lugging your vacuum around a lot. Does it feel right when you use it? How heavy is it? Picture yourself using it in a four-story house—with carpeted stairways—at the end of a very long day.
- **Cord length.** The longer, the better.
- **Noise.** Is it too loud for you or your clients?

Do some research, and shop around. The Internet is chock-full of vacuum information. A specialty vacuum store is also a good place to start; the salespeople will be able to answer your questions and help you find the machine that's right for you.

- **Wood cleaner** for wooden floors, cupboards, wainscoting, baseboards, and other wood surfaces.
- **Brushes and/or scrub pads.** You can either choose a utility brush and a mini brush (soft bristles will prevent scratches), or use nylon scrubbing pads.
- **Feather or lamb's wool duster.**
- **Cleaning cloths.** Don't use synthetic fibers; natural terry cloths or cotton dusting cloths are far better. Make sure the cloth is electrostatic and lint-free. You can also purchase lint-free paper towels.
- **Dust formula.** Apply this to your cleaning cloths and your dry mop.
- **Dry mop.** These are generally much better than brooms for initial floor cleanup. A broom just moves the dirt around the floor, but dirt and dust particles will cling to a dry mop.
- **Wet mop and mop bucket.** Some cleaners swear by sponge mops, others by string heads. See what works best for you. In general, the sponge types are more convenient for small areas; string mops for larger floors.
- **Gloves.** If your hands are sensitive, these can be lifesavers.

A Cleaning Play-by-Play

Cleaning technique is, of course, a very individual matter. Everyone cleans a little differently, and there is really no right or wrong way. Still, there are a few tricks of the trade that might help you out, or at least give you something to think about. Chances are you'll agree with some and disagree intensely with others. That's fine! The right method is the one that works best for you.

Most cleaners would agree, however, that in this business, time is money. The more quickly you can clean a house—without sacrificing thoroughness—the more jobs you can fit into a day, and the more money you can earn. If you can complete the basics more quickly, you'll also have time to offer clients little extra touches that will keep them coming back. So how can you be most efficient? Here are some tips:

- **Make the most of every movement.** You can save an amazing amount of time by simply paying a little attention to your movements. You want to avoid backtracking: Remember, each footstep spent retrieving the can of cleanser you left in another room costs you time and energy.

- **Work around a room in a circle,** clockwise or counterclockwise, whatever works best for you. You'll minimize footsteps and be less likely to leave any tasks out.
- **Work from top to bottom.** You don't want to reclean surfaces that your cleaning process itself messed up.
- **Clean dry, then clean wet.** You want to remove dirt and dust before applying any cleaning solution.
- **Let your products work for you.** After you apply a cleaning solution, give it a few minutes to work before rinsing it off.
- **Have the supplies you need at hand.** It's best to carry them with you in a caddy or your cleaning apron.
- **Keep tools and equipment in good working order.** Rinse your brushes at the end of a job. Throw cleaning cloths into the washing machine at the end of the day; do the same with dust mops periodically. Change your vacuum cleaner bags and filters regularly.

Where do you start cleaning? Naturally, you don't want to be tracking new dirt into rooms you've already cleaned, so it's most efficient to start with the least central rooms: usually bathrooms and bedrooms. Save the kitchen and other high-traffic areas for last.

Bathroom

- Clean the tub/shower from top to bottom with an all-purpose or disinfectant cleaner; be careful to use nothing abrasive on fiberglass. Ceramic tile may call for a scrubbing brush or pad. Glass shower doors can be cleaned with glass cleaner. Don't forget to check the door runners and clean with a brush and paper towels if needed. It's a good idea to put a cloth or paper towels down on the floor; you can stand on these while you clean to avoid tracking dirt into the tub.
- Clean the toilet bowl first with disinfectant or toilet bowl cleaner; let the cleaner do its work for a few minutes, then brush and flush. Next, clean the seat and other surfaces by spraying with disinfectant cleaner, letting it stand, and wiping with a cloth or paper towels.

- Clean the mirror with glass cleaner and lint-free paper towels.
- Wipe the walls and light switches.
- Spray the countertop with disinfectant or all-purpose cleaner and wipe it dry.
- Clean the sink and faucets with disinfectant or all-purpose cleaner and wipe dry.
- Cleaning the soap dish is an extra touch that bigger companies don't do but clients appreciate.
- Finally, dry-mop the floor, then wet-mop or wax it.

Living Room, Bedrooms, and Similar Areas

Living rooms, family rooms, dens, offices, bedrooms . . . all these rooms involve the same sorts of cleaning tasks.

Some cleaners dust and swipe before they vacuum (on the theory that the dust will fall to the floor, where it can then be vacuumed away); others vacuum before they dust (because the vacuum stirs up dust in the room, which the dusting will then take away). If your vacuum is top-notch, you'll probably want to at least give the dust-first method a try. If you're using an older model (or a client's older model), it's worth keeping the vacuum-first method in mind. As always, the right method is whatever works best for you.

- When you dust, move around the room, starting high and moving down. Paintings and bookshelves might come first, for instance, followed by tabletops.
- Anytime you use dust formula, apply it to your cloth, not to the surface you are cleaning.
- A TV screen can be gone over with an electrostatic cloth. You can also spray glass cleaner onto a cleaning cloth (never onto the screen), wipe the screen, then dry it.
- Don't forget to give electrical switchplates a once-over. They're inevitably covered with fingerprints.
- It's better to vacuum slowly and thoroughly than to go over the same floor again and again.
- Vacuum systematically. It can be helpful to divide a large room into sections and move from one to the next.

Stairways

Wooden stairs can be dry-mopped. Work from the top down.

Carpeted stairs *can* be vacuumed with an upright vacuum; working from the top down may be easier on your back. You might prefer to do this job with a canister vacuum, however, or with a mini vac. Whatever you do, be careful not to let the cord get in the way.

Kitchen

The order in which you clean the kitchen will be determined by its floor plan. As always, work around the room, from top to bottom.

- Clean any countertop appliances: Remove crumbs from the toaster oven and clean it; clean the microwave inside and out. (Specialized cleaners are available for this, or you can use a mild all-purpose cleaner.)
- Clean the countertops with an all-purpose or disinfectant cleaner. Remember to move appliances out of the way and clean underneath them as well.
- Clean the stovetop with an all-purpose or disinfectant cleaner.
- Wipe down the refrigerator, oven, dishwasher, washing machine, and dryer with all-purpose or glass cleaner.
- Clean the sink with a nonabrasive all-purpose or disinfectant cleaner, or a specialized cleaner for the particular surface. Let the cleaner sit for a few minutes before rinsing; then wipe the sink dry with a lint-free cloth or paper towel.
- Finally, dry-mop the floor, then wet-mop or wax it.

Scheduling

You'll want to find a balance between a schedule that meets your own needs and one that meets your clients' needs. You might need to be more flexible as you start out; once you're in demand, you'll likely have a waiting list, and that gives you more control over your time.

You will have a schedule disaster at some point in your business: An unexpected crisis—small or large—can ruin the best-laid plans, bad weather could throw a wrench into things, or you might simply be overly optimistic about your timetable. There's nothing to do but muddle through as best you can, trusting your clients' understanding, perhaps offering reduced rates or makeup visits—and learning from the experience. Here are some other things to think about as you start to set up a housekeeping schedule:

- How many houses can you reasonably clean in a day? Some cleaners cheerfully take on three or four jobs a day; others are worn out after a single home. Don't try to do more than you can complete and feel good about.
- Take transportation time into account. How far is it between the homes you clean? Leave adequate time to get from one house to another. You may also need time to stop at a gas station, convenience store, or bank between jobs.
- How much extra time do you want to allow yourself in the schedule? If you leave yourself an hour to get from house to house when it generally takes only forty minutes, you'll feel more relaxed and in control. On the other hand, you may wish to maximize your number of jobs by having a tighter schedule.
- Remember time for meals, snacks, and breaks. Some cleaners are happy to eat in the car between jobs; others prefer to wait until they're done for the day; and still others like a set lunch break, allowing them a chance to unwind for a while. Think about how you'll be happiest, and schedule this time into each workday.
- We all have errands and appointments that we need to take care of from time to time. You might need to see your doctor, accountant, lawyer, or printer during business hours. It's wise to have an open hour or two during each week for such events.
- Don't forget to allow time for administrative work: record keeping, filing, answering e-mail, returning phone calls, and so on.
- Breakdowns in scheduling happen to all of us, no matter how long we've been in business. Have a plan for dealing with these, and set it down in writing in your service manual. It's also wise to have client contact information close at hand wherever you go. If a scheduling problem comes up during the day, you'll know how to reach your clients to let them know.

Taking Care of Yourself

Having a solid support system is critical if you're starting a business. We've said it before, but it's worth repeating: You'll be working harder for yourself than you *ever* worked for anyone else. And you'll want—you'll need—people out there who can help you cope with all the new demands you'll be facing.

If you're lacking in the support department, think about ways you might fill in the gaps. Are there friends from the past you can reconnect with? Family members who've been there for you before? Support groups you can join or create? Even cleaning newsgroups and forums on the Internet can remind you that you're not alone. (Just be careful on the Net; you can't trust everyone or everything there.) Or perhaps a church, synagogue, or other spiritual group can provide you with connections and encouragement.

Don't forget to take time for yourself. What makes you feel special: a gourmet meal, a day off, a hot bath, a walk in the woods? Give it to yourself. Are you an animal lover? Visit your local humane society and spend an hour hugging the dogs and cats; you'll all benefit. (You may even be able to volunteer as an official cuddler.) And you can always try bartering your housecleaning services for those of a massage therapist!

Here are some other tips that might help you feel good through a long and successful housecleaning career:

- **Take care of your feet.** You will be on your feet for a large part of every day, so it's worth investing in shoes that are comfortable and offer your feet the support they need. What kind of shoes is up to you: athletic shoes, walking shoes, work shoes, or even soft slippers. There are a lot of great choices out there, and you should get what works best and is most comfortable for you. Go to a good shoe store and talk to the folks there about their recommendations. Make sure to give them a realistic picture of the demands you place on your feet.
- **Wear comfortable clothes.** Forget the latest fashions; what you need is clothing you can move in, not to mention lift, stretch, bend, and sweat in.
- **Watch how you lift.** If nothing else, you'll be lifting a vacuum cleaner a lot on this job, and chances are you'll be lifting other weights too. Learn how to lift things safely, with your lower body, not your back. If you've ever injured your back even

slightly, you'll understand how important this is. Even a tiny sprain can put you out of commission for weeks.

- **Watch for reactions to the products you use.** You'll be exposed to cleaning products more than most people are, so watch out for any adverse reactions you might have to them. You can also try using hypoallergenic and scent-free products; many cleaners prefer these (and so do many clients). Remember to wear good-quality rubber gloves.

- **Take time off.** That's tough to do as an entrepreneur. You do have to sacrifice a lot of free time when you're starting up a new business venture, but don't sacrifice all of it. You need some downtime to relax, to reinvigorate yourself, to spend time with loved ones, to remind yourself what you're in business *for.* Find a balance that works right for you. It might mean guaranteeing yourself one full day off a week. It might mean taking a week off twice a year. It might mean unplugging the phone in the evening. Whatever *"time off"* means to you, you need it just as much as you need your clients and your sponges.

- **Watch for signs of burnout.** Being crabby and irritable all the time, feeling out of control of your emotions or moods, experiencing sleep disorders (maybe you want to sleep all the time, or maybe you find yourself lying awake all night), losing interest in your work (or your family or friends), receiving complaints about the job you're doing: All of these are warning signs that scream *Lighten up!* Listen to them. Your career is on the line. Burnout can leave you out of commission forever.

- **Eat right.** You've heard this one before, but it's true. Having the right nutrients to keep your body fueled can be critical to getting through your demanding day. Eating regular, healthy, nonsugary meals and snacks will make you feel better and work better. (Still, every now and then "eating right" *can* include a hot fudge sundae when you really, really need it.)

- **Music** can be a great tool for staying sane. If you're alone while you clean, you might be able to bring along a cassette player or radio and listen to music you enjoy (just be sure the volume is low enough that you don't disturb the neighbors). Or you might enjoy listening to books on tape. If this isn't possible while you're cleaning, make sure you have plenty to listen to in the car while you're driving from job to job. Some people find that music can make administrative and record-keeping work a pleasure rather than a chore.

The Victorian Housemaid

In Victorian times, if there was a dirty job to do, the housemaid was the one to do it. The housemaid was responsible for most of the dirty and backbreaking tasks that kept the household running. She was usually under the direct supervision of the house-keeper. In the early morning she swept the whole of the downstairs rooms; cleaned and raked out the grates in the fireplaces, removing the dead ashes and kindling from the night before; polished the grates; then laid a new fire in preparation for the day ahead. She also carried numerous heavy buckets of water upstairs, not only so that the household members could bathe, but also to do her daily chores with. Then she changed the bed linens, got rid of any fleas, lice, bedbugs, or other unwelcome guests, then made the beds again. The upstairs received a thorough scrubbing. The housemaid also mended any household linen in need of repair.

- **Exercise.** Yes, cleaning houses is demanding physical work, but it doesn't really qualify as aerobic exercise, the kind that keeps your heart and lungs and muscles healthy. Try to work some aerobic exercise into your weekly routine. Even going for walks can make a huge difference. You might enjoy swimming or bicycling—exercises you can do without being on your feet. Do be realistic, though. If you're feeling fatigued, sleep is probably more important than exercise. Your doctor or health care provider can help you find a balance that's right for you.

- Speaking of **sleep,** make sure to do it! Everyone's sleep needs differ. If you're not used to being active all day, you might find that your sleep needs increase when you begin a housecleaning career. Pay attention to your body; if you're not get-ting enough sleep, it will let you know.

- **Stress reduction techniques** might help you too. Breathing techniques, yoga, meditation, visualization—all these can help you stay healthy and happy. It might all sound very New Agey, but it doesn't have to be. Breathing exercises can be about finding a spiritual center, but they can also serve as a simple relaxation technique; it's up to you. Investigate your local bookstores, the Internet, and community resources for information on dealing with stress. You'll find a lot of good workshops, classes, seminars, books, and much more out there for you.

Chapter Seven

Understanding and Serving Customers

The housecleaning field requires a sense of dedication and a true commitment to customer service. Because you will be relying heavily on word of mouth to advertise your business, excellent customer service is mandatory. Without it, your business may never get off the ground.

The key to customer service is to remember that all of us are customers ourselves. Think about some of the businesses and services that you frequent and why. You might choose to do business at a bank that has slightly higher fees than others nearby, for instance, because of the way you're treated: You're always greeted with a smile, and the banking representatives, who know you by name, ask how business is going and how the weather's treating you. Such interactions can make you feel like not simply a customer, but also a friend.

The more you know about your clients, the better you'll be able to service them. Just remembering names and addresses isn't enough in this day and age. You should always know your clients' cleaning needs, of course, but remembering some personal information will serve you well too. Putting that extra touch into your business dealings will go a long way toward keeping your clients happy, and it will help you cultivate new clients as well.

Making clients feel special helps establish trust, a vital ingredient in any entrepreneurial endeavor. It also establishes your credibility, because clients will be much more comfortable knowing that you don't think of them just as a job to be done. Moreover, a client who's happy and feels that you care will lead you to other potential clients. Your ability to provide excellent customer service can be the key to building your business into a successful and prosperous one. (Some sample client information records are included in chapter 9.)

First impressions are usually long-lasting ones. From your initial consultation on, the better you present yourself, the better your company will look to prospective customers. Pay attention to details: Notice the sort of decorations and artwork in a client's home, for example. If you make the client feel that her or his home is special, the client will have a better feeling about you coming in to clean it.

Melinda's Story

I keep a card file with client information: birth dates, pets' names, children's names, known medical issues, job title, and any special holidays they observe. This gives me the opportunity to personally congratulate clients on job promotions; wish them a happy birthday, a pleasant Rosh Hashanah, or a happy Easter; and inquire about their health. I have several clients with seasonal allergies, and I often inquire as to whether or not the pollen is more severe this year than last; little things like that go a long way toward making people feel they're more than just paying clients.

Smith, Michael (born April 3)

Spouse: Mary (born May 19)

Children: Joshua David (born October 6, 1993); Zoe Claire (born December 22, 1995)

Pets: Sam (black Labrador retriever; outdoor only)

Occupation: Michael: civil engineer, town of Larchmont. Mary: pediatrician, Family Care Services.

Allergies: Michael: cats. Joshua: dust, pollen, lactose, peanuts, various other foods. Zoe: peanuts.

Health concerns: Joshua: asthma.

Hobbies: Michael: sailing, model ships. Mary: sailing, knitting. Joshua: stamp collecting.

Special concerns: Joshua's room needs careful attention to dust. Mary often leaves files and journals lying around; these shouldn't be disturbed. Ask Zoe about her ballet lessons.

Five Essential Elements of Customer Service

1. Be courteous and friendly.

This should be a given, but many people can go an entire day without doing this. Being courteous and friendly costs you nothing and will go a long way toward making customers happy—not only with you, but also with the service you have provided. A friendly and courteous manner helps establish trust and generates understanding between you and your customers.

2. Stay focused on your customers.

When you are with customers, always maintain eye contact. Not only does this imply honesty, but it also shows respect. Don't do other things—turning your back, washing your hands—while engaged in a conversation with a client. Yes, you're there to provide a service, but you're also there to pay attention to the client. Treat each client as if she or he is your only client.

3. Ask questions.

You won't be able to offer outstanding customer service unless you're able to determine what the customer expects. You can help your customers outline their specific needs by asking specific questions of them. Talk to them about their needs and preferences. Give them different options and help them find what will work best for them. Does the client prefer that you leave the toilet seats down, or that you not open the windows while working? Think about how you'd like to perform the assignment, and get feedback from the client.

4. Listen to your customers.

Now that you have asked the questions, you need to listen to the answers given to you. Pay close attention to the client's responses, write them down, and use this information to help your customers get what they want. Offer your advice and expertise, but don't talk over the client. You have to put your active listening skills to work! If you don't understand, then ask for clarification. This way you'll both have a clear understanding of the services that will be provided.

5. Follow through on your service.

No matter how courteous and friendly you are, no matter how focused you may be, regardless of how many questions you might have asked, and no matter how long and hard you have listened, none of this will matter if you don't follow through with your client. If you say that you'll have the house plan completed by Friday, be sure that it's completed and delivered to the client on Friday. Keeping your promises is the most important aspect of excellent customer service, and yet the most overlooked. If you offered a special service, be sure the customer receives it. Not to do so is the surest and quickest way to become unemployed!

These five elements are not all that's encompassed by the term *customer service,* but they are indeed essential. Without these five ingredients, your service will fall flat.

Recite the five essential guidelines as a mantra. When the going gets tough, and a client is being uncooperative, recite your mantra. Do what it takes (within reason, of course) to keep a client happy. A happy customer will usually spread the word to others seeking the same dependable, reliable, and exceptional service that you have provided. All it takes is some dedication on your part and a commitment to treating others the way you would expect to be treated.

Take the time to know your customers. Laugh with them and enjoy their company. Be genuine and show that your company cares about them, not just as customers but as individuals as well. And remember to smile!

Chapter Eight

Setting Up the Home Office

Home offices are found in basements, attics, spare rooms, dining rooms, and even walk-in closets. An extra bedroom or den area is ideal, but with some creativity you can create a workable space in the corner of a room that is currently being used. You might even convert a pantry into your home office. Wherever you set up, though, there are some things you'll need.

Basic Equipment

All well-stocked housecleaners should have the following items—eventually. You might not be able to afford all of them right away, and that's OK. A computer, in particular, can be both expensive and intimidating. It will be worth the time and energy you put into acquiring it and learning to use it; we can guarantee that. But don't feel that you can't begin cleaning clients' homes until you have a computer (or the other equipment listed here). It will be more complicated, but it can be done.

Separate Phone Line with Voice Mail

Having a dedicated business line is a must! An extra phone line costs about $25 a month. When clients are telephoning, you don't want your personal answering machine to pick up the call, nor do you want small children answering the phone. Solve problems before they start by getting a separate telephone line with voice mail; either buy an answering machine or have voice mail added to your regular telephone service. Also, be sure the telephone jack is located near your desk space. You don't want to have to get up out of your chair and walk to another room to answer your business line. (A portable phone would work too.) Leave your voice mail on whenever you aren't at your desk.

Large Table or Computer Armoire

You needn't invest in a big, expensive desk. People are always attracted to large desks with lots of drawers. The drawers, however, encourage clutter and take up too much valuable space for a small area. A table is a much better choice. You might find something at a secondhand store; if the surface is in poor condition, paint over it with a high-gloss paint or simply cover it with an attractive tablecloth. The table must be sturdy enough to hold a computer and a few accessories, and tall enough to fit some metal file cabinets beneath. Be sure that the table you purchase is lightweight, so that you'll be able to move it if you need to.

The desk area should be large enough to accommodate your entire setup: phone, computer components, printer, and scanner. I wouldn't spend more than $100 for a table. If you can't find anything for less than $100, try a home improvement store that has a lumber department. You can purchase a huge unfinished wooden tabletop nearly 4 inches thick for about $40. You can stain or paint it, and support the corners atop four metal storage cabinets. Throw a tablecloth over it, and no one will ever know the difference.

Armoires are terrific pieces of office furniture—like an office on wheels! Armoires are simply tall cabinets, much like a wardrobe or standing cabinet. The inside is carefully fitted with compartments to house your computer setup. Some even have a pullout table for writing, thus eliminating the need for a desk or table. The downside is that they can be expensive, starting at around $400 and ranging up to a few thousand dollars. Sometimes you can find them in secondhand stores, as well as in the classifieds. The advantage of using an armoire is that once you close the door, you've closed the office.

Comfortable Chair

You'll be spending considerable time sitting and doing administrative work, so you need a comfortable chair. Comfort and cost go hand in hand, so avoid the bargain chairs. There's nothing worse than working at a computer for two hours while sitting in a chair that has no back or lumbar support. The next day your back will let you know that it's not pleased with you!

You can sometimes find great deals on chairs at thrift stores or used office furniture stores. Be sure to get lumbar support, and think about choosing a chair that rolls easily on the surface of your floor. The less expensive chairs don't roll easily. If you have carpeting in your home office, you'll need a special hard plastic mat under the rolling chair. This prevents your carpet from being damaged. Similarly, if you have hardwood floors, a rubber mat will protect the floor and prevent the chair from rolling out of control.

Be sure to select a model that can be adjusted easily, both in height and in back position; a simple lever is ideal. With some of the less expensive chairs, you need a screwdriver to adjust the height—not very convenient. The chair's back should adjust to allow you to sit back or straight up.

A good chair will cost about $125 brand new. The investment is worth it!

File Cabinets

One or two locking filing cabinets should be sufficient. Lightweight metal cabinets are easy to clean, and they can be emptied and moved with little effort. It's important to keep paper file copies as backups to your computer disk or CD-ROM copies. If your computer ever goes on the blink, you'll be able to refer to the paper copies. You are dealing with confidential information (for instance, you probably have the codes to your clients' home burglar alarms), so it's best to lock the paper copies and the disks or CD-ROMs inside the filing cabinets. If anyone enters your office, she or he won't be able to open the cabinet and go through the files. The tricky part is finding a safe place to store file cabinet keys. It's a good idea to have two sets, hidden in two separate places. Don't hide keys in a desk drawer, under a desk plant, or under the keyboard. Those are the first places a would-be burglar will look!

Fireproof Safe

A safe is a must because you'll be storing client's house keys, and clients need to know that these keys are secure. For even more security, be sure that your safe is fireproof. Although nothing is 100 percent fireproof, most models will withstand temperatures of 1,850 degrees

Fahrenheit for two hours. You can purchase a small fireproof safe with a combination or key lock for around $120. I don't recommend the electronic touch-pad models; they're expensive, starting at around $350, and if something goes wrong with the keyboard, you can't access the safe. If you have a combination or key lock safe and something happens to the locks, you can always call a locksmith.

Never get into the habit of leaving clients' keys on your table or desk or in your car. Keep the keys locked in the safe at all times when not in use. Make a habit of going to the safe the minute you walk in the door.

A medium-size safe works best. Small safes can easily be picked up and carried away should your home ever be burglarized. Safes can be covered with a tablecloth and used as a table; no one need ever know what's beneath it. You could also put the safe in the back of a closet. Keep it out of sight of windows and doors. People should be able to sit in or walk around your office and never see the safe. Wall models are terrific: The safe is set into the wall and covered by a picture. Given the cost of the safe itself—upward of $500—and the cost of installation, however, wall safes are out of reach for most people.

Combination locks can be difficult if you're in a hurry. The more hurried you are, the more often you'll stop at the wrong number or turn the dial in the wrong direction, resulting in frustration. Key locks are easiest, providing that you've hidden the key in a memorable place. Never store the keys to the safe with clients' house keys or your personal keys. It's just too easy to lose them.

Computer

The biggest purchase that you'll make—if you don't own one already—is a home computer. If you're in the market for a computer, don't be dazzled by all the bells and whistles. For your business, a basic model will do just as well as the higher-priced ones. Monitor size is a matter of personal preference; some people like larger monitors, but a smaller model can be a great space saver. Expect to spend anywhere from $700 to $1,200 for a basic computer. Do stick with a name brand; unfamiliar manufacturers come and go, while the familiar brands have customer service divisions to help you if you ever have a problem.

I've found it better to use a PC than a Mac. The two systems are in many ways incompatible, and more households and businesses use PCs than Macs.

Once you select a computer and set it up, you'll want to choose an Internet service provider (ISP). Chapter 12 will tell you all you need to know about using the Web in your business. You can generate a huge amount of business as a result of your Web presence.

Color Printer

These days you can purchase an efficient color ink jet printer for $80 to $150. Black ink replacement cartridges cost between $15 and $25; color cartridges run $25 to $35, depending on the manufacturer. The cartridges last for a few thousand copies. Both cartridges usually last about five months if you typically print fifty or so pages a day. You can use a color printer to print:

- flyers
- business cards
- your *Guide to Services*
- billing statements
- letters
- and just about anything else!

If you need to print an item in quantities of more than 200, it's less time-consuming to have an office supply store run off the copies on a high-speed copier, but if you have the time, it's also quite doable on an ink jet. Laser jet printers are becoming popular due to their high print quality, but they're very expensive and not necessary for your housecleaning business. We've never been able to tell the difference between a document printed on an ink jet and one printed on a laser jet.

Scanner

A scanner is another accessory that has come way down in price over the past few years. A good scanner can be purchased these days for around $100. A scanner also works as a copy machine; it's ideal for making a few copies of signed contract pages, forms, receipts, and so forth. You can either scan a printable copy, or you can scan copies to a disk or CD-ROM, virtually eliminating excess paper filing. You will also be able to use the scanner to scan photos onto your Web site.

When comparing scanners, look for the user-friendliest models. These have features such as a one-button copier (a great time-saving shortcut) or a one-touch scanning button. Most scanners are compatible with any model of PC. Ask a salesperson and research the brands in *Consumer's Digest* or a similar product guide.

Other Supplies to Keep on Hand

- 8½-by-11-inch paper puncher. This allows you to keep your documents and service manuals in three-ring binders.
- Stapler.
- Pens and pencils.
- Disks or CD-ROMs and storage case.
- Dry erase board to use as a calendar.
- Copy paper.
- Paper recycling bin.
- Index cards and storage box.
- Rolodex.

Privacy

Once you set up your workspace, make it clear to your household and family members that the space is absolutely off limits to anyone except you. At no time should a spouse, friend, or child be in the office. The office is a place to conduct business and nothing else. Instruct household and family members that when you are in your office, you are not to be disturbed. This means children, friends, family, neighbors—everyone! This can be tough for household members who think of you as *being* home and not *working* from home. Try hanging a DO NOT DISTURB sign on the door.

Boundaries

Treat your home business as you would any other professional place of business. This means setting business hours for yourself. Give yourself a schedule—every day from 6:00 to 8:00 A.M., for example. Then stick to it. You should spend the time in your office dealing with administrative tasks, planning, marketing, reading business literature, and so forth. When the scheduled time is over, get up and leave the office space. Don't be tempted to make personal telephone calls or catch up on personal correspondence during business hours.

The Victorian Scullery Maid

A scullery maid's day was spent mostly in the kitchen. Working under the supervision and direction of the cook, her duties fell to washing all dishes, pots, and pans. She also blackened and lighted the stoves in the mornings and cleaned the scullery, larders, kitchen, and servants' quarters. She was responsible for keeping the entire kitchen area clean and free from any rodents that might be present in the larder.

Combining business with your personal affairs can be a trap. Likewise, don't take family time or personal time to take care of business. You may have to experiment with several types of work schedules until you find one that works for you.

Chapter Nine

Record Keeping

L ike cleaning itself, record keeping is a bit of an individual affair; only you know exactly what procedures will work best for you. There are, however, some minimum records that you must keep for tax purposes. Know that the more detailed your records, the better off you'll be.

Expense reports allow you to analyze your spending in detail and discover how you can save money: Perhaps you're paying for advertising that doesn't work, or maybe your car maintenance bills are heftier than they ought to be.

Income records give you a clear picture of the money you have available to you at any moment, and the money you can expect to receive. They also help you keep track of late payments and discover patterns in clients' payment histories. All this information is vital if you want to have a complete picture of your business.

As a small start-up, record keeping should be fairly simple and straightforward. If you take out a loan at any point in the future, however, banks will need detailed business records. And if you decide to become an employer, detailed record keeping will be a legal necessity. For all these reasons, good record keeping is a habit well worth getting into from the very beginning.

Client records are important in this business as well. The more you know and remember about your clients—their needs, their interests, their quirks, their preferences— the better you can serve them. Clients are trusting you with their homes, their possessions, their keys. It's vital that you have contact information for clients, police, poison control, home alarm system providers, and the like at your fingertips at all times.

So where do you begin? This chapter contains some sample records for a housecleaning business; they may offer you a starting point. There are excellent software programs and manual accounting systems, available at stationery or office supply stores, that will set you up with all the records you need.

Cash or Accrual?

The first decision you'll need to make as you begin keeping business records is whether to use the cash system or the accrual system. You must choose one or the other and use it consistently.

In the cash system, you record each payment that you receive when you receive it; you record each expense when you pay it. If you bill a client on January 1 and she doesn't pay you until January 18, you record the transaction in your accounts on January 18. If you buy supplies via credit card, taking home your purchases on January 10 but not actually paying your credit card bill until January 25, you record the expense as occurring on January 25.

The accrual system involves recording payments and expenses on the date the transaction occurred, rather than the date that the money was actually paid or received. If you use the accrual system and bill a client on January 1, you'd list the payment in your records as occurring on January 1. The supplies you took home on January 10 would be listed on January 10.

Of the two systems, cash is the simpler. You keep your records much the way you maintain your checkbook register. Unless you maintain a large inventory (unlikely as a housecleaner) or extend credit to your clients (ditto), we recommend the cash system. If you use an accountant or bookkeeper, however, it's worth finding out her or his opinion on the question. Your adviser knows your own situation best.

The Business Checkbook

Your business checkbook is your first line of record-keeping defense. Remember to use your account only for business purposes. Reconcile your account against your bank statement every month. Not only will you stay on top of your income and expenses, but you'll be able to catch any errors and correct them quickly.

Mileage Records

Chances are you'll be using your car to drive from cleaning job to cleaning job. If you do, you'll need to keep track of *all* your business mileage: every mile, every fraction of a mile. As you'll see in chapter 10, there are two different ways to record automobile expenses and deduct them from your taxable income, but both of them require you to have a mileage record. If you don't write it down, you can't claim it as a deduction. Miles quickly add up to dollars at tax time.

Your best bet is to keep a small notebook right in your car; the glove compartment is a good home for it. Make a habit out of writing down the beginning mileage at the start of every business trip, no matter how short. When you reach your destination, write down the closing mileage. You can do the math right on the spot, if you like, or save this task for later; the important part is to get your mileage written down. If you car has a trip counter, a special odometer than can be reset at the start of each journey, by all means use it and save yourself some time!

Income Records

Your income is the payments received from clients. You can record this information on a simple chart; a sample is below. For each payment, you should record the client's name, the invoice date, the date you received payment, and the payment type (if it's by check, record the check number as well). Also, save any and all documentation verifying your income: your bank statements, credit card documents, on-line payment records, and so on. Keep all these documents in their own spot: a file in your filing cabinet, a basket on your desk, even a shoe box. The point is to have *all* your documents in one safe place.

Expense Records

Expenses are a little more complicated than income, but not a lot. First of all, you should know that there are three types of business expenses: direct, indirect, and capital. *Direct expenses* are what the IRS calls "ordinary and necessary" costs, the stuff you have to pay for simply to run a business. They include cleaning supplies, office supplies, transportation expenses, advertising, and so on. These are the expenses you'll want to keep close track of.

					Pmt. Type (including	
Inv. #	Date	Client	Amt.	Date Paid	check #)	Comments

Sample Record: Income

Inv. #	Date	Client	Amt.	Date Paid	Pmt. Type (including check #)	Comments

Again, you'll want to keep documentation (sales receipts, canceled checks, credit card statements) for all your direct expenses, and these documents should be stored in their own separate, safe place. You should also record each expense in an expense ledger, either on paper or on a computer spreadsheet. For a start-up cleaning business, it's probably adequate to do this recording once a month; if you expand, however, and especially if you hire employees, you might want to keep weekly records.

Indirect expenses are the costs of running your home office, based on the percentage of your home that you use. Chapter 10 has all the information you need to calculate your indirect expenses. In brief, if 10 percent of your house (based on square footage) is used as

Sample Record: Direct Business Expenses						
	Jan	Feb	Mar	Apr	May	Year
Advertising						
display ads						
flyers						
other						
Auto						
gas						
tolls						
maintenance						
insurance						
other						
Insurance						
liability insurance						
bonding						
Professional services						
legal						
accounting						
other						
Office expenses						
Internet service						
telephone						
cell phone						
business cards						
office supplies						
merchant acc't fees						
checking acc't fees						
Cleaning supplies						
Cleaning equipment						
License fees						
Other expenses						
Total expenses						

your home office, you can then deduct 10 percent of your house expenses from your taxable income; these expenses would include rent or mortgage, insurance, heat, electricity, and so on. As a cleaning business, you can calculate these expenses once a year (or have your accountant or tax preparer do so) to include on your tax returns. You could keep records of these expenses every month—and of course, it's not a bad idea to do so!—but as a small service provider, this is probably overkill.

Capital expenses are incurred when you purchase expensive equipment that will serve your business for many years. As a cleaner, this would most likely include your computer and vacuum cleaner. Rather than deducting the entire cost of such a purchase from your taxable income in the year you bought it, you'd want to deduct the cost of a year's worth of use, also known as depreciation. Your tax preparer can provide you with information about depreciation.

For your purposes, then, expense records should focus on direct expenses; you and your tax preparer will worry about indirect and capital expenses at tax time. Above is a sample of a monthly direct business expense record you might use. The more detailed you can be in categorizing your expenses, the more useful the information will be. You might want to break down the Telephone category, for instance, into basic service charges, long-distance fees, voice-mail system, and fax. If your telephone bill is of concern to you (maybe it's just too high, or maybe it suddenly shoots up one month), having such detailed records will help you analyze the problem and figure out how to solve it.

To keep up to date with your expense reports, sit down once a month and go through all of the invoices and other expense documentation that you've set aside in its special place. Categorize each payment, then add them up and insert them on this form. You've now got a simple at-a-glance picture of where your money goes. Add the monthly totals to get the yearly figure when preparing your tax return.

Monthly Net Income Statement

Once you have monthly income and expense records, you can compare the two in a simple income statement. For the purposes of a housecleaning business, a simple statement like the one shown here should give you a picture of your business's health.

```
┌─────────────────────────────────────────────────────────────┐
│         Sample Record: Monthly Net Income Statement           │
│                                                               │
│                  total receipts      $_____                  │
│                                                               │
│              – total expenses        $_____                  │
│                                                               │
│                  = net income        $_____                  │
│                                                               │
│            – estimated taxes         $_____                  │
│                                                               │
│               = actual income        $_____                  │
│                                                               │
└─────────────────────────────────────────────────────────────┘
```

Client Records

As we've noted in chapter 7, having client information available at your fingertips can be invaluable to your business. You'll be able to give top-notch customer service by reminding yourself of each client's preferences, special dates, and family members. And you'll always know how to reach the client and anyone else you need to contact if a problem arises.

Following are some sample client records.

Invoicing

There are many ways to invoice clients, from an understanding that a check will be left on the kitchen counter every week (be sure to get this agreement in writing) to weekly or monthly statements. You can find invoice forms at office supply and stationery stores, or purchase software that helps you create your own. Following is a sample invoice that might be helpful.

John Burns, 456 Green Street

E-mail address _____   Work telephone _____

Home telephone _____   Cell phone _____

Home alarm system _____ yes _____ no

Home alarm system code and instructions _____

Telephone number of home alarm system provider _____

Dates valid: _____ through _____

Emergency Information

Telephone number of contractor or repair person _____

Cell phone number of contractor or repair person _____

Alternate Key Holders

Name _____   Name _____

Address _____   Address _____

Telephone _____   Telephone _____

Cell phone _____   Cell phone _____

Relationship to client _____   Relationship to client _____

Telephone and Account Numbers (where applicable)

Gas company _____

Electric company _____

Water bureau _____

Telephone company _____

Fire department _____

Police department _____

Poison control _____

Sample Client Record, Page 1

Service and Payment Record

Client _____

Date	Hours	Amt. Due	Date Billed	Invoice #	Date paid	Comments

Sample Client Record, Page 2

Colonial Village Cleaners

123 Brownstone Street

Cleveland, Ohio 12345

(123) 555–1234

Invoice number _____

Date _____

Client name and address

_____

_____

_____

_____

Services: **Amount Due:**

_____   _____

_____   _____

_____   _____

_____   _____

_____   _____

_____   _____

                    Total: _____

Payment is due within 14 days.

Sample Invoice

Chapter Ten
Taxes

Operating your own business and working for a business are two entirely different experiences. When you work for a company, the only tax issue you need to deal with is ensuring that your state and federal taxes are being withheld at the appropriate rate. When you own a business, however, the mere mention of taxation can be a bit intimidating. Sometimes new business owners fall into the trap of thinking that they don't need to follow business tax regulations. Often, the owner of a start-up will wait to turn a profit before showing this on her or his tax returns. That's a big no-no.

As a self-employed business owner, you'll be paying taxes not once a year but quarterly: Every three months, you'll send both the state and federal governments a check covering your estimated tax bill for that period. The estimates are based on your previous year's income, and at the end of each tax year you reconcile the estimated payments you made with the actual income you ended up receiving. If you overpaid, you'll get a refund; if you underpaid, you'll send in what you owe. You don't get any bills or statements from the government reminding you of your quarterly tax obligation; it's up to you to send it in, and if you don't, you can face some stiff penalties and nasty surprises come April 15. Your accountant or tax preparer can help you with all of this, and you can also get information from the Small Business Administration or the IRS (see the list of resources in Appendix II).

Deductions for the Home-Based Business

In order to be eligible for home-business-related tax deductions, the Internal Revenue Service requires that the specific portion of your home that you are going to claim as a business deduction be used *regularly and exclusively* for business. This is the principal location of your business or a place you have reserved to meet prospective customers and conduct office administration. The location may not be used to entertain family members or to store personal belongings. Any equipment that you claim, such as a telephone or computer, must also be used exclusively for business purposes.

In order for your business to qualify under the *exclusive use* test, you must be using the deductible portion of your home for only business-related activities. This area can be a separate room or other clearly defined area of your home. It does not have to be marked off by a permanent partition of any kind.

> *Example:* Let's say that your dining room doubles as a home office. Three or four times a week, you use your dining room as a place to prepare customer billing statements, review contracts, and read industry journals. Your family also uses this room for meals. The dining room is then not considered to be an exclusive home office, and therefore it cannot be used to claim a business deduction.

In order for your business to qualify under the *regular use* test, you must be using a specific area of your home for business on a regular basis. You will not meet the test if the business use of the area is only incidental or occasional, even if you don't use it for any other reason.

> *Example:* Suppose you use a specific part of your home, such as a spare bedroom, to regularly view promotional videotapes on stock market variations, investment strategies, and trends. You don't, however, actually invest in the market or otherwise participate in the opportunities described in the tapes. Because these activities are not part of your regular business function, you cannot claim a business deduction for the business use of your spare room.

As your business grows, you may have other business locations in addition to your home. In order to qualify for a business deduction for the use of your home, you must be able to meet the *principal place of business* test. Your home office may qualify as your principal place of business for deducting certain expenses if you meet the following criteria:

- You use your home office for administrative or managerial activities for your business exclusively and regularly.

- Your home office is the only fixed area in which you regularly and exclusively conduct substantial administrative or managerial activities.

On the other hand, if you use the home office for your business exclusively and regularly, but your home office does not qualify as your principal location for business based on the above rules, you can establish your principal place of business based on the relative importance of the activities performed and the function served at each location, or the time spent at each location.

If your home office cannot be identified as your principal place of business, you won't be able to claim it as an expense. There may still be other ways for you to deduct home office expenses, however.

If you regularly meet or greet clients or customers in a part of your home throughout the normal course of your business—even though you generally conduct your business at another location or locations—you may be able to deduct expenses for that part of your home. That portion must be used exclusively and regularly for business, and qualifies for a deduction if

- you actually meet clients or customers on your premises.
- the use of your home is an integral and substantial part of the way in which you conduct your business.

The occasional use of your home for business meetings and business-related phone calls would not qualify you for a deduction of the expenses for the business part of your home.

You may also deduct the expenses for a separate structure, such as a garage or shed, if it's freestanding and you use it for the exclusive and regular use of your business. This structure does not have to be your principal place of business or a place where you meet clients or customers.

Example: Albert Jones operates a candle shop in town. He makes the candles in a garage behind his house. Because Mr. Jones only uses the garage exclusively and regularly for his candle making business, he will be able to deduct the expenses for the use of the garage.

Once you have met the criteria for qualifying for deductions, you can then figure out how much you can deduct. You must determine the percentage of your home used for your business. There are two commonly used methods:

- Divide the area that's used for business (length multiplied by width) by the total area of your home.
- Divide the number of rooms used for your business by the total number of rooms in the house. You can use this method as long as your rooms are all of comparable size.

You won't be able to deduct the business expense of your home office for times when you did not use your home office for business purposes or endeavors. For example, if you set up your home business on July 1, when it comes time to calculate your yearly allowable tax deductions, you must begin in the calendar month that the business was launched—in this case, July. You cannot claim expenses from the beginning of the calendar year.

Remember, the Internal Revenue Service is going to be treating the part of your home that you use for business as though it were a separate entity, a separate piece of property. What this means to the home-business owner is that meticulous records must be kept. There should be no mixing of business and personal receipts. All business receipts and logs need to be kept separate. There is no one method that is required, but your records must clearly justify the deductions that you'll be claiming for your home business. Claiming home-business deductions does not automatically instigate an audit of your tax return. Still, it's always wise to keep thorough records and to stay well within the boundaries set up to qualify for home-business deductions. Consult a tax specialist or other similar expert in this field when managing this particular aspect of your business.

Deductions for the Housecleaning Business

Generally, in order to be eligible for business deductions, you must be engaged in an activity with the intent to make a profit. In order to meet this requirement, your business must show a profit in any two years of a five-year period. You may also take business deductions for such things as supplies, subscriptions to business-related journals and publications, an allowance for the business use of your car, insurance, and other related expenses.

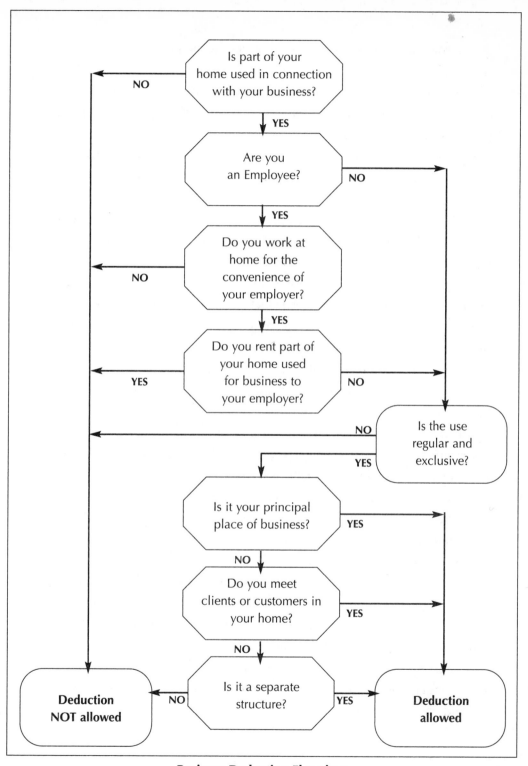

Business Deduction Flowchart

Let's take a look at some common business deductions:

- **Advertising.** These expenses include ads placed in the yellow pages, newspaper ads, and magnetic car signs, as well as the costs of printing flyers and business cards (see chapter 12).
- **Automobile expenses.** You can either deduct your actual automobile expenses or use a standard mileage rate. Both methods require you to keep track of your business mileage.

    The actual-expense method works like this: First, determine what percentage of your car use is for the business. For example, if you put 12,000 miles on your car last year, and have documented 6,000 miles traveled for your house-cleaning business, then 50 percent of your vehicle use was business related (6,000÷12,000 = .50). You can now deduct 50 percent of your car expenses from your taxable income. This includes all expenses: license and registration fees, insurance, maintenance, repairs, tolls, parking, and gasoline. (Of course, you will have kept meticulous records of all these expenses, and kept invoices and other documents supporting them; see chapter 9.) This is the more complicated method, but it can add up to a larger deduction.

    The standard mileage method involves simply documenting how many miles you travel for business purposes, then multiplying this mileage by a standard rate that's announced annually by the IRS. At this writing, the rate was 34.5 cents per mile. If you drove 6,000 miles for business purposes, your deduction would be $2,070 (6,000 x .345). All you need to document in this method is the actual mileage. If you use the standard mileage rate, you cannot deduct auto expenses separately; they're included in the rate.
- **Cellular phone.** If 50 percent or more of your phone usage is for business-related calls, you can elect to fully deduct the business portion of the purchase price in the year the phone was bought. If less than 50 percent of its use is for business, you must instead use straight-line depreciation.
- **Clothing.** Clothing that's required for your business that cannot also be used outside of business hours is deductible as a miscellaneous item deduction. The laundry and cleaning expenses involved for qualified clothing are also deductible.

Such articles of clothing would include uniforms, safety shoes, and safety goggles. Jeans, even if used exclusively for your job, are not deductible.

- **Computer expenses.** The business parts of your home computer and any peripheral hardware or software equipment are deductible on Schedule C if you own a sole proprietorship. If the computer was bought for business use, you'll be able to deduct the business portion of the purchase price. If 50 percent or more of the computer usage is for business-related activities, you can elect to fully deduct the business portion of the purchase price in the year the computer was bought. If less than 50 percent of its use is for business, you must instead use straight-line depreciation.

- **Health insurance.** If you are self-employed, you may deduct up to a certain percent of your health insurance payments from your gross income on page one of Form 1040. Check with the IRS or your tax preparer for the exact percentage, which is subject to change.

- **Home office.** A deduction for your home office is available for your business if you use a portion of your home according to the criteria described earlier.

- **Internet expenses.** Internet expenses related to your business can be deducted on Schedule C and Schedule A as miscellaneous deductions.

- **Licenses.** Licenses related to your business may be deductible on Schedule C or Schedule A.

- **Subscriptions.** Magazine and trade journal subscriptions, as well as newspapers and books, may be deductible if they're related to your business.

- **Telephone expenses.** Only phone calls that are related to your business, investments, or jobs may be deducted. The cost of a primary phone line isn't deductible; it's presumed that this is for personal use. A second line for business, however, or additional phone services such as call waiting and call forwarding, may be deductible.

Chapter Eleven
Insurance and Bonding

In today's lawsuit-happy culture, no business can afford to be uninsured. Likewise, an in-home service provider should carry a surety bond, also known as a dishonesty bond, to cover incidents of theft. Of course, you're not stealing anything yourself; but anyone at any time can claim that a household item is missing and point a finger at anyone with access to the house. You can also be sued for any number of offenses, real or imagined. Therefore, it's critical that you understand how liability and bonding work, to save yourself a lot of anxiety and headaches down the road.

Liability Insurance

Liability insurance is protection for yourself, your income, your home, and any other property that you own should a client slap you with a lawsuit. You might think, *I'm only cleaning houses; what could I possibly be sued for?* The answer is *quite a bit*. Because you're going into someone's home to provide a service, you can be sued for damage to or theft of any item in that home, as well as damage to the building structure itself. Legal representation can cost more money than you'll make in two years' time, and you still have to pay the legal fees even if you're found not guilty.

The most common lawsuit is for damages to the client's property. The obvious damages to someone's property are usually accidental. Breakage, for instance, is something that happens to the best of us, usually through no fault of our own. Perhaps you go to open a window blind and the entire fixture crashes to the floor, breaking a table lamp in the process. Or maybe a client has crowded glass or ceramic items so tightly together that you break one while trying to pick it up and dust it. During your in-home consultation, you should always carefully evaluate such areas. It could easily take several hours to safely and responsibly clean the items in a china cabinet.

You could also be sued for damages that result from tracking mud or engine grease onto a client's Oriental carpet. Or you might be held responsible for the damages caused by using the wrong products, even if the label stated that the product was suitable for the surface you used it on. Major problems such as structural damage to the building or water and fire damage could be your responsibility. Or suppose you leave a door unlocked and someone comes in and ransacks the place—again, you're up the creek. Seasoned cleaners as well as newcomers to the trade often think, *It won't happen to me*. Never say never! Over the years we've collected several lawsuit horror stories from other cleaners.

- One cleaner slipped on a child's toy that was on the kitchen floor, accidentally putting a hole in the plaster wall with the handle of the broom she was holding. (Remember, just because something is an accident doesn't mean you're not responsible for the damages.) The client never asked the cleaner to repair the hole in the plaster; he simply slapped her with a suit for close to $10,000, which included replacement of the entire wall. You might think that the presence of the toy on the floor was the client's fault—which it was—but it never occurred to the cleaner to file a countersuit. The client argued that it was less expensive to replace the wall than to patch and paint it. The figure also included the cost of replacing the toy that was damaged when the cleaner stepped on it, as well as compensation for the personal suffering that the client endured by having to look at a wall with a hole in it for a while. He also argued that he used his home for business meetings, but was unable to use the room where the damage occurred from the time that the hole appeared until the wall was replaced, a period of six weeks. He claimed business losses, and was awarded the judgment. Fortunately, the cleaner had liability insurance. Although she only had to pay her $250 deductible, that's still a lot of money for something that wasn't really her fault.
- Another cleaner was accused of having left an upstairs bathroom sink faucet running with the sink stopper in place; no one noticed it for a day and a half. The family was alerted when the second floor, which had become waterlogged, crashed into the first floor. The cleaner argued that she'd never even turned on

the faucet in that bathroom. She was hit with a $60,000 lawsuit to cover the cost of the repair, as well as temporary housing in a first-class hotel suite for the family from the day the damage occurred until the repair was completed (three months).

The case is still in litigation. The lawyer for the cleaner's insurance company brought up a valid point: Within the home resided three children, all under the age of five, who were roaming the house unsupervised during the time that the cleaner was there. This is another reason not to work when unsupervised children or other people are present in the home, and another argument for having liability insurance!

- A cleaner had her purse stolen from her locked car while she was in the local movie theater. The purse contained a key ring with all of her clients' house keys. All eleven of the clients' homes had to be rekeyed, at the cost of nearly $400 per home. The housecleaner had no insurance, and she was not able to pay the incurred charges. Some of the clients are in litigation with their homeowner's insurance providers, and some of those providers have refused to pay. Consequently, the clients have filed suit. This cleaner will eventually have to make restitution to the clients, which she can't afford to do. She has subsequently lost her business and her reputation, a nightmare that could easily have been avoided by purchasing even a minimal liability policy.

Always maintain a liability insurance policy. It's inexpensive, and you'll be known as a reputable service provider. Put yourself in the client's shoes: Would you want an uninsured person coming into your home and handling heirlooms, expensive china, costly crystal, or collectible artwork? Or mopping your $20,000 marble floor with the wrong product? Would you consider going to a medical doctor or auto mechanic who wasn't insured?

On the other hand, you must always be on the alert for people who might try to pull off an insurance scam. It happens every day. That kindly middle-aged mother of four who hired you to help with household chores because she was overwhelmed could be setting you up to take the fall for fictitious damage or theft. Such people make a sizable living from insurance fraud. Like any other criminal, there's no special look to these characters, and often there's no desperate or bizarre motive other than figuring out how to get away with a moneymaking insurance scam.

During your first consultation, be on the alert if someone asks for explicit details about insurance coverage: liability amounts, renewal dates, and so forth. All the information that clients need is contained in your service manual: your policy number, and the name and telephone number of the insurance company, so that they may call the company to confirm your coverage.

There are a couple of ways to go about getting liability insurance for your cleaning business. If you already have insurance for a car, or homeowner's or renter's insurance, call the agent who handles those policies. Because you're already a customer, you'll generally be offered a frequent user or multiple policy rate, usually 10 to 15 percent off all your policies. You can also do an Internet search for business liability insurance. There are probably 150 to 200 companies that write policies specifically for small businesses. Most of the Web sources have an on-line form that you fill out and submit, and an agent contacts you via e-mail with a quote. The rates are usually very reasonable. Avoid giving out your telephone number for insurance quotes; salespeople pitching the latest insurance plan will bombard you.

Insurance rates differ depending on the state, county, town, township, or city that you live in. The ballpark figure for general liability insurance varies from $250 to about $400 a year. The following sample outlines a very basic general liability policy:

Sample Certificate Limits of Liability

$1,000,000	Each occurrence
$2,000,000	General aggregate limit
$1,000,000	Product/completed operations limit
$1,000,000	Personal and advertising injury limit
$50,000	Fire damage limit
$5,000	Medical payments
$10,000	Care, custody, and control
$10,000	Key loss
Deductible:	$250 bodily injury/property damage deductible per claim (including loss adjustment expense)

Before we move on and discuss bonding, let's break down the legal language.

Each Occurrence

An occurrence is each single claim or loss. If a person tries to sue you, the most your insurance company would pay is $1 million—highly unlikely unless you've wreaked total disaster on a million-dollar mansion.

General Aggregate Limit

The general aggregate is the maximum amount of losses that the insurance company will cover during the policy period. In the example shown, the insurance company would pay no more than $2 million during the policy period. (Usually a policy period is one year from the date that you requested and paid for the policy.) If this is part of the policy you purchase, two people at two separate residences could sue you for a million dollars each, or four people could sue you for $500,000 each. In any case, once you hit the $2 million point for one policy year, the insurance company would pay no more. Again, being sued for millions by several people is highly unlikely.

Product/Completed Operations Limit

This coverage isn't really helpful to cleaners, but it's part of any standard liability policy. It simply offers protection from lawsuits that stem from anything you sell or give to your clients. Say, for instance, that you invent a new all-purpose cleaner. You give the product to a client to try, and when she uses it on a glass tabletop, the product chemically reacts with the old product's residue. The new product ignites, starting a fire that damages everything in the room. You'd have plenty of coverage for such an episode. Obviously, you should never give or sell products as part of your cleaning service. Products that you bring to the client's home to use are different (they would be covered as damages) from those you give a client to use.

Personal and Advertising Injury Limit

Advertising injury involves making a statement in your advertising that leads to loss by another person or business through libel, slander, defamation, the violation of the right to privacy, theft of ideas, or infringement of copyright, trademark, title, or slogan. Personal injury, in this case, refers to injuries (damage) that the other person or company claims as a result of your alleged violation. This sort of lawsuit might be filed if you lift ideas, logos, ad copy, and so forth from another person's advertising forum, or if you slander another company and the company loses business because of your comment.

Fire Damage and Medical Payments

These are pretty self-explanatory. If you cause a fire, the general policy will cover up to $50,000 in damage. Fires are rare; as a housecleaner, you shouldn't have any reason to light a flame. After all, you're cleaning, not cooking. A medical payments clause would cover a client for injury suffered—for instance, a client who's hurt when attempting to use your homemade cleaning product, or one who stops by your home to drop off your check and slips on the ice on the sidewalk. You've got $5,000 worth of medical coverage to use for such a client. This is medical coverage for *other people* who are physically hurt or injured as a result of your negligence; it is not medical coverage for you. In the case of a serious injury that might cost more than $5,000, the client is covered under her or his medical and/or homeowner's insurance; that's why the general coverage is low. If you're worried about this, you can purchase additional coverage for a small fee.

Care, Custody, and Control

This is part of the general liability policy that is infrequently used. It covers property that is temporarily placed in your possession. *Temporarily* is the key word. If you agreed to care for a rare plant for a client who was planning a lengthy vacation, for instance, and the plant died, you'd be covered. Still, you won't have to worry about this clause if you set boundaries with your clients. Accept no other duty or responsibility other than the housecleaning work that you contracted to do.

Key Loss

If you ever lose a client's keys, this clause will be your saving grace. To avoid having to fall back on this coverage, follow responsible security standards by locking all keys in a safe when they're not in use.

Do you see how you can get burned by giving in to requests for work that has nothing to do with housecleaning? You might simply agree to turn on the teakettle and end up with a million-dollar lawsuit. As we've pointed out in previous sections of this book, always think carefully about accepting a job if the client or other people are going to be in the house. Someone could easily trip over the electric cord to the vacuum cleaner (the cord that *you* plugged in), break a leg, and then sue *you* for negligence. It happens every day, and you can't afford to think it can't happen to you.

Bonding

General liability polices don't cover theft; for this, you need to purchase a surety bond. These are inexpensive—around $50 per $5,000 of coverage—and are good for one year. The bond covers litigation costs and the value of the stolen item (up to the amount of the bond purchased) if you are convicted of the crime. A client can accuse you of stealing a $20,000 Rolex watch from his jewelry box, for instance, but not much will come out of such an accusation unless he can prove it. He'd need to have some pretty incriminating evidence, or a reliable witness to the crime. Without these, he'd have to present a case built on circumstantial evidence.

If an item turns up missing, you cannot be convicted simply because you were in the home, or because you have a key to the house. These sorts of claims rarely go anywhere because theft is very difficult to prove. Still, paying the $50 bond fee is worth the money because it sends out the message that you are a professional who does not take risks. Bonding is the mark of a reputable business. It also dissuades scam artists from making fraudulent claims.

Surety bonds are available through most insurance companies. If the provider of your liability policy doesn't offer these bonds, your agent should be able to refer you to a firm that does. There are also dozens of bond providers that advertise on the Internet. If you conduct a search, however, be sure to use the term *surety bond,* otherwise you'll get a list of thousands of people who provide bail bonds (to spring people out of jail), which have nothing to do with surety bonds.

It's fairly easy to secure a bond. The form asks for basic information: name of the company, address, and so forth. It also asks if you've been convicted of a crime within the past seven years. If you have been convicted, answer truthfully. A yes answer doesn't mean automatic denial, especially if you were convicted of something minor, such as not paying parking tickets. If you are unable to be bonded because of a criminal conviction, there isn't much you can do except shop around. Some bonding companies will take the risk; others won't.

If at some point you decide to hire an independent contractor to work for your company, you will need to purchase liability coverage for that person. This changes your policy from that of a sole proprietor to a standard policyholder, and the rates will increase by about 60 percent. You will also need to purchase a surety bond for each employee. Most sole proprietor insurance polices and bonds will automatically extend to include a spouse, free of charge, but neither the policy nor the bond covers anyone else.

If you advertise your company as being insured and bonded, be sure to keep the coverage up to date. The last thing you need is a lawsuit and an expired policy. If you feel that the general liability policies have inadequate limits, you can purchase additional limits for a small fee. If you do in fact work in an area where homes are valued at $25 million—Beverly Hills, Bel Air, Palm Springs—it won't hurt you to up your coverage!

Chapter Twelve
Advertising

A dvertising is the most important component of building a profitable business. Still, with so many choices available for new businesses, it's hard to know where to start and how much money to set aside for advertising. You could spend as little as $10 or as much as $1,500 and get the same results. Advertising for a one-person cleaning business is far different from the strategy that an operation with fifteen employees would use. It isn't worth your while—at least not at first—to invest in a huge, expensive advertising package.

To develop an effective advertising strategy, you need a pretty good idea of your expected business growth. Most cleaners are satisfied with operating a one-person business and want nothing to do with hiring employees or serving hundreds of clients. There's nothing wrong with such a choice; in fact, this is how the majority of cleaning businesses prefer to operate. On the other hand, a few owners are interested in immediate growth, expansion of services, and higher profits. Either choice will make a great impact on how you go about choosing advertising forums.

For now, let's assume that your company will function with you as the sole employee. Because there's only so much business that you can accommodate, it doesn't make much sense to spend an entire year's projected salary on an advertising package that will generate more business than you can handle. Turning away hordes of potential clients will only cause aggravation, both for you and for the folks inquiring about services.

What sort of advertising works best? Let's take a closer look at your choices.

The Web

The Internet is your best selling tool. It's inexpensive and delivers up-to-the-minute information. Today's consumers are Web savvy, and a vast majority of American households have computers. Getting a Web site is easy: If your Internet service provider (ISP) provides a free home page, your site can be up and running within twenty-four hours. The Web site can answer almost any question that potential customers might have before they even pick up the phone.

To set up a Web site of your own, begin by registering your domain name. On a search engine, type in *domain name* or *domain registration;* you'll get thousands of possibilities. Look through ten or twenty of them and compare prices. Three of the most popular domain registries that have been around for quite a while are

- www.registernames.com
- www.ICDomainnames.com
- www.networksolutions.com

Because the domain registries are competing against each other, they try to come up with a variety of package plans, discounts, and specials. At times these options can be as confusing as choosing a long-distance provider. The basic plan includes simply the use of the domain name and Web forwarding; this is all you really need. The total price for a one-year package runs between $20 and $40.

You're then ready to set up your Web site. If your ISP offers free home pages, you're in business. AOL has a user-friendly Web page building tool called HomeTown; other ISPs have similar features.

Melinda's Story

Since I developed and launched my Web site two years ago, I haven't had to run a single newspaper ad. The site is linked to my ISP home page; I pay a yearly fee of $35 for my domain name and a Web forwarding function. The Web page lists my zones and services. If customers like what they see, they can download my service guide to read and review it. Then they can e-mail or phone for further information or to set up a consultation. It's a great way to do business: You weed out the folks who aren't willing to pay your rates, and the frequently asked questions are answered before you even pick up the phone. And you can't beat the cost! I'd estimate that 95 percent of my new customers come to me as a result of my Web presence.

If you don't like the Web tools available through your ISP, or if the provider charges you for home pages, you can still build a free Web site. There are many companies on the Web that provide free pages. All of them come with advertising in the form of pop-ups, clickable icons, banners, and so on. Compare the sites to see which is the least annoying to you and—more importantly—to your customers. Here are some recommended Web page providers:

- Geocites.com (owned by Yahoo!)
- Angelfire.com
- Hypermart.com
- Freetown.com
- Dreamwater.com
- MSN.com
- Tripod.Lycos.com

Your Web site itself should be clean, clutter-free, professional, and easy to navigate and maintain. The simplest structure to use is a three-page site. This gives you enough space to describe your business without clutter. The first page, the home page, will give basic information: company name, mission statement, and an icon that people can click to read about your services. The second page, Services, provides a brief description of what you offer as well as an opportunity to request your *Guide to Services.* The third page, a photo gallery, gives potential clients a visual sampling of your work.

This is indeed the age of the Internet; can you afford *not* to be on the Web?

Yellow Pages

The yellow pages work well for large corporations, but not so well for small businesses. An average yellow page listing costs between $700 and $3,000 a year. The larger the city or town, the higher the fee. It simply isn't worth the yearly gain of two or three clients. Furthermore, what happens once your business takes off and your time slots are filled? There your yellow page ad will sit, attracting new customers whom you'll have to disappoint.

Newspapers

Newspapers are by far one of the least expensive and most effective ways of getting the word out. Because you're a small company that serves a specific locale, an ad in the smallest community paper of that area will start the ball rolling. Be sure to limit your ads to those newspapers serving the zones you actually work in!

Display Ads

Display ads are far better than classified ads. People are much more apt to notice and remember display ads than text. You don't need fancy graphics; your simple black-on-white business card will be just fine.

Before you purchase a display ad, leaf through the newspaper and select two or three sections where you'd like your ad inserted. Newspapers will charge a small additional fee if you request that your ad be placed in a specific section of the paper. It's worth it. A display ad placed in the family section, among ads for children's activities and day care services, is likely to generate much more business than one placed next to advertisements for funeral homes and florists.

Classified Ads

Classified ads are becoming a thing of the past. They can be very expensive; some periodicals charge as much as $2.00 to $3.00 a word, with a twenty-five-word minimum. They generate less business now than they did years ago, simply because of the increase in Web shopping. You could, however, gain clients rather inexpensively by placing a carefully worded classified ad in a community newspaper.

We don't recommend placing advertising in those small weekly publications that are geared exclusively toward classifieds. We don't know of any housecleaners who have had an ounce of luck with them, and you probably won't either; the people who read them are usually in the market for cars or furniture, not household services. Save your money to advertise in a regular newspaper.

Flyers

Flyers can be tempting: They're relatively easy and inexpensive to produce, and can be distributed quickly and easily. In truth, however, more people will throw them away than will actually read them. Let's see what works and what doesn't.

If you're like most people, you've probably received dozens of flyers on your car windshield over the years, and you've probably been more angered than interested. Many homes have a NO SOLICITATION sign on the door, or a decal that states NO HANDBILLS OR FLYERS. If you ignore the resident's wishes, you could be issued a citation. This is especially true in apartment and condo buildings, which often have strict rules against solicitation. It's also against federal law to place anything in a mailbox.

One solution is the doorknob hanger. Blank doorknob hangers can be purchased in office supply stores for around fifty cents apiece. They're made of thick card stock and are far more attractive than mass-photocopied flyers. You can print them on your home computer and be selective about where you hang them. For instance, wherever you see a moving truck or a HOUSE FOR SALE sign, place a hanger on the doorknob. Folks just moving into a neighborhood will likely be interested in the services available in their new community. Furthermore, someone who is moving out may need help cleaning the home and preparing it for the new tenant. Keep your eye out for new housing developments. They are prime candidates! You could feasibly sign up an entire neighborhood in a week's time.

with.

I was wrong. I received only two calls about my ad, both inappropriate. So I kept thinking. The next ad I ran read: "Housecleaning services available weekdays 10 A.M.–2 P.M. Call 555–1234."

I received three calls on the ad's first day. One caller hired me to clean twice a week. A second wanted to reserve every Monday because no one ever had openings on Mondays. The third caller reserved my services every other Friday.

The moral of the story is: If you're going to place a classified ad, be as specific as you can. In my case, being specific about my hours was the key to attracting customers. You're paying for each printed word, so get as much for your money as you can!

...ards

...ome without one!

...me you have reason to mention your occupation, take advantage of the opportu...to hand out a business card. Did you know that within a twenty-four-hour period, ...probably mention your occupation at least seven times? And think about all the community bulletin boards you see in your daily life. Each one is free advertising! Take advantage especially of bulletin boards located where busy people convene or are running errands:

- Supermarkets and health food stores
- Gyms and weight loss centers
- Schools and community centers
- Hospitals (people recovering from surgery or childbirth might desperately need your services!)
- Libraries
- Veterinary offices
- Churches
- Day spas

Busy, active people are all potential clients. Whenever you can, you want to place a business card either in the hands of these people or at eye level in the places they frequent.

Business cards are inexpensive. You can have them professionally printed by an offset printing house by the thousands for about $200. The simplest and least expensive business card to produce is one that includes a simple black-on-white logo, a one-sentence motto or affirmation, and your telephone number or Web address. If you choose to include colors, you'll be paying more: Expect the price to go up at least $175 *per color* for each 1,000 cards.

Most printers will print a run of 1,000 cards with a one-time setup fee of about $50. The setup fee is charged because the printer has to make a plate of your card—something like a large metal mold. The plate is stored with the printing house; anytime you need more cards, the plate is pulled and the cards printed. Be aware, though, that some printers have a minimum print run of 5,000 cards or more. Many printing houses on the Internet advertise incredibly inexpensive print runs. You'll want to look at these carefully; when you factor in the postage, the cost often exceeds what the printer down the street might charge. Large print runs can set you back around $1,000 if you don't shop around.

You can also buy sheets of blank business cards to print from your home computer. Blank cards are available at office supply stores in packages of 100 to 500. A 100-card package costs about $15, and the business card software can run anywhere from $10 to $50. There are advantages and disadvantages to printing your own cards. On the plus side, it's far less expensive than commercial printing if you have a simple logo on a disk or CD-ROM. Disk or CD-ROM storage allows you to upload the logo image to the business card software. You can have your cards printed and ready to go in about thirty minutes. Even the no-frills, least complicated business card software includes a hefty selection of font and print styles to choose from. The higher-end software contains hundreds of styles. You can choose to print the cards all at once or only as needed. You can also experiment with different card designs: vertical or horizontal logo placement, bold text, and so forth. You're not bound to any one design; if you don't like what you've developed, you can change it and create a totally different card in less than ten minutes.

The downside is that if you use colors, you'll go through ink cartridges quickly, and color cartridges are expensive. Also, although the cards are perforated for easy separation, you've got to be careful. If you pull too hard, you can easily damage the cards, resulting in waste.

Magnetic Car Signs

I like to think of magnetic car signs as business cards for cars! They're inexpensive head turners. Magnetic car signs, which can be made by a multifunctional printer, usually come in pairs (one for the driver's side door and one for the passenger's side) and cost between $50 and $100. There are many graphic artists who specialize in magnetic signs and who advertise on the Internet. The most economical and useful sign is simply text on a white background. You need only the name of your business, perhaps a short phrase such as *Housecleaning by Appointment,* and your Web address or telephone number.

Make sure the signs are on your car at all times, and especially when you're parked in high-traffic areas such as supermarket parking lots. When you're parked at clients' homes, too, neighbors will take notice. You'll be amazed not only at the number of inquiries but also at how many of those inquiries turn into jobs! Because the signs are magnetic, they're easy to remove anytime you prefer not to display them.

Networking

Networking is the oldest form of advertising. Centuries ago, proprietors advertised via word of mouth only; there were no phone books or newspapers. Today, despite mass media, community networking remains a resourceful and reliable plan for getting the word out about your business. And it's free! To be included in a network of service providers is an honor that must be earned, so don't be surprised if it takes several months to start making connections.

To make it easier, be the first to approach other professional service providers. Such folks can include:

- wedding planners
- pet-sitters
- interior decorators
- child care providers
- lawn care workers
- visiting nurses and home health care aides
- errand-running services

E-mail or telephone the other provider and explain a little bit about your company: the types of clients you serve, your zones of service, availability, a rough example of rates, and so forth. Ask if you can exchange flyers or business cards. Have a large index card available to write down contact information about the other provider and her or his company. Offer to recommend the provider's services should you ever receive an inquiry, and ask the other provider to do the same. Clients usually feel better about hiring someone based on a personal referral. As a housecleaner, then, the next time you're asked about lawn mowing, you can go to your file and pull out the name, Web address, or phone number of someone who provides that service. Clients will be thrilled, and you will be too when other providers offer your name to folks inquiring about housecleaning services.

Word of Mouth

The very best advertising is free—and it's priceless. If you do good work, your own clients will sell your services for you. There are housecleaners out there who have never advertised in any way. One client told a friend ... who told a friend ... who told a friend ... and within a matter of months, the cleaners had waiting lists.

Provide superior service, and the world will come to you!

Fund-raising and Community Outreach

Get involved in your community by donating your time and services at least once a month. Not only is volunteering a great humanitarian effort, it's fun and a great way to advertise for free. Find a cause that you're interested in. If time is an issue for you, you can make a small monetary contribution in the name of your business. It's tax deductible, and the charity will be grateful. Here are some examples of creative volunteering:

- Help sponsor community events: blood drives, walkathons, car washes, pet adoptions. The name of your business will appear in a newsletter or on television, or it will be posted in a public area.
- Donate your services to a nursing home, hospice, library, or shelter. You'll be helping needy folks, and the employees and coordinators of the institutions will come to see you as an honorable person representing a terrific business—and will likely recommend your services to others.
- Donate a small amount to public television or radio station fund-raisers. They always mention the names of contributors on the air.
- Donate your services to fund-raising auctions. As part of a fund-raising auction for a local women's shelter, one housecleaner donated two hours of cleaning, which was purchased for $450! At the time, two hours of cleaning was a $45 value, so the women's shelter received $450, the benefactor got a clean house, and the cleaner got a $45 tax deduction and referrals to several new clients.
- Organize your own event. Get together with other service providers and pick up trash in a schoolyard or public park. Call the local newspapers to come out and interview you and take photographs.

No matter how little or how much you give, when you help charitable causes, you can't lose.

Advertising Options at a Glance

Medium	Cost	Effectiveness	Comments
The Web	Low-cost: $30–50 per month	Extremely effective	Highly recommended. It's possible to generate almost all of your business through the Internet.
Yellow pages	Expensive: $700–$3,000 per year	Not effective	Chances are you won't get clients when you want them, and you'll get too many when you don't.
Newspaper display ad	Low-cost	Very effective	Pay attention to your ad's placement if you want it to be effective.
Classified ad	Fairly expensive: $50–$150 per ad	Somewhat effective	Be as specific about your services as possible for the best response.
Flyers	Relatively inexpensive	Somewhat effective	For best results, target your flyers. People buying or selling a home make good candidates. Flyers broadcast indiscriminately get little response.
Business cards	Low-cost to fairly expensive	Very effective	Don't leave home without them!
Magnetic car sign	Low-cost: $50–$100	Very effective	Business cards for cars.
Networking	Free	Very effective	Having a network of service providers to recommend to your clients benefits everyone—and it's free.
Community outreach	Free	Very effective	Generate both new clients and goodwill for your business, and do something worthwhile for your community too.

Chapter Thirteen

When Bad Things Happen to Good Housecleaners

Here's a secret not many people want to talk about: There are some scary people out there. As a housecleaner, you're going to meet some of them. At some point in your career you may find yourself frustrated, angry, insulted, even downright shocked. It's an occupational hazard. This section is about how to keep your sanity, hold your head up, soar with dignity, and handle the scary situations.

How do you know when a prospective or present client is behaving inappropriately? How do you recognize on-the-job stress? What do you do about it?

Inappropriate behavior or abuse can be either overt or covert. Overt is the easier to recognize. It may take the form of yelling; of any sort of physical gesture, including slamming doors, snapping fingers, or shoving; or of chastising you for drinking water or using the bathroom. It's any behavior that humiliates you, and you will recognize it instantly.

Covert abuse is more subtle, and the dividing lines are fuzzier. Is it abusive when someone conducts an inappropriate conversation with family members while you're in the home: yelling at a child, screaming at a spouse, scolding others, including other service providers or employees? How about someone who pumps you for personal information? ("Are you on welfare? What's your religion?") Or a client who refers to you as "the help" or "the girl"? Asks personal questions about other clients? Makes racist, sexist, or otherwise offensive remarks?

Ultimately, these are questions you'll have to answer for yourself. We can tell you this: Pay attention to your instincts. Any behavior that makes you feel uncomfortable deserves a very close look.

So what do you do when faced with an uncomfortable situation, overt or covert? After all, you can't very well tell people how to behave in their own homes. What you can do is to remember that you are first and foremost a human being. Second, you are a professional, and as a self-employed professional, you don't have the luxury of reporting inappropriate behavior to higher-ups. You are your own Division of Human Resources, and you must deal with the problem directly.

When things go awry, get out of the situation immediately. Pretending that it doesn't bother you or feeling that you have to put up with poor treatment only perpetuates it. Don't allow second chances for people who degrade you. There is no job worth being humiliated for.

After you've left the situation—walked off the job—let the person know that you've done so because you refuse to tolerate the behavior or comments. It's not always safe to do this face to face; you never know what the other person is going to do. You don't want to end up with a mop thrown at you, or worse. Once you're out of there, however, you can write a short note that details why you left, and mail it to the client. You're not going to change anyone's beliefs or prejudices overnight, but you've at least done the right thing by sending out the message that such behavior is unacceptable.

It's important to structure every housecleaning in detail, right from the beginning. Remember the service manual and room plans from chapter 4? These take a long time to complete, but they're critical. They let everyone know what to expect from you.

College professors often spend the first day of each class handing out and reviewing the course syllabus, the key to passing the class. The syllabus lists what is expected and what will happen if the work is not completed at the scheduled time. It includes due dates for reading assignments, quiz and test schedules, presentation dates, and grading criteria. Studying and following the syllabus almost guarantees a high grade.

Your service manual and room plans are the syllabus of your housecleaning business. Structuring every detail of a housecleaning is a lengthy process, but an investment well worth the time. Your manual can save you from some pretty scary situations and people. If a client is put off by your structure, then you're not the right service provider for her or him.

The Victorian Housekeeper

A century ago, many servants accompanied their employers when they traveled between residences, but the housekeeper generally stayed at the main house, overseeing the order and the overall cleanliness of the household and keeping it in a state of readiness for the employers' return. She was also responsible for all linen (except the table linen), and the estate or house stores: sugar, flour, spices, soaps, and candles. The housekeeper was also charged with keeping the premises free from both rot and vermin. Some made distilled waters from rose, lavender, or lilac, along with soaps and basic medicines for the household's use. Finally, the housekeeper oversaw the yearly spring cleaning, when the house was scrubbed from top to bottom.

You are responsible for maintaining your dignity, self-esteem, and sense of worth. No one can give you dignity, but they can certainly take it away. Choose assignments that will enable you to be valued and rewarded for doing a good job. Remember, you're not just a service provider but also the service *regulator*. You're in the driver's seat!

Chapter Fourteen
The Future

Your housecleaning business is limited only by your own imagination. Once you've established yourself and your reputation, you can take your career anywhere you want to go!

Becoming an Employer

If your waiting list is longer than your client list, or if you're simply longing for new challenges, it may be time to expand your business by taking on employees. Becoming an employer is an enormous sea change in your business, and not something to consider lightly. It's also a far larger subject than can be dealt with thoroughly in a volume like this.

If you have employees, you must know and adhere to all the laws and regulations governing employers, including the Equal Employment Opportunity Act, National Labor Relations Act, Age Discrimination in Employment Act, Americans with Disabilities Act, Drug Free Workplace Act, and many others. You also need to know and adhere to all IRS regulations governing employers. This includes verifying each employee's eligibility to work, withholding taxes from her or his paycheck, and keeping on top of all IRS-required paperwork.

Before you hire your first employee, you'll also want to answer these questions:

- What hours will your employee(s) work? What vacation days will you offer? What about sick and/or personal days?

- How much will you pay your employees? How often will you review their work and offer promotions or raises? What criteria will you use to evaluate employees' work?
- What benefits will you offer—health insurance, pension plans, tuition assistance?
- How will you deal with grievances? With employee discipline?
- What will be your policy regarding substance abuse? Sexual harassment?
- What other personnel policies are important to you? Think, for instance, about clothing, eating or smoking on the job, tardiness, confidential information (relating to either clients or your business), use of business or clients' resources for personal activities, and so forth.

You'll also have to deal with recruiting potential employees, interviewing them (this includes complying with all laws and regulations governing nondiscrimination in hiring—for instance, you can't ask a potential employee her or his age or marital status), training them, and sometimes firing them.

And these are just some of the issues you'll have to consider. Clearly, taking on employees can be a full-time job in itself. But if you love dealing with people, have a hearty appetite for administrative work, and want to grow your business, it offers many challenges and rewards. If you're interested, a great first step is to talk to the people at the Small Business Administration (see the list of resources in Appendix II).

Becoming a Specialist

As you gain experience in your housecleaning business, you might find that particular aspects of the job intrigue you. You may be able to grow your business by specializing in areas you really love. Many cleaners, for instance, offer nontoxic, ecofriendly cleaning products and services; this can be a selling point for your business, and clients will be willing to pay more for your work if they know they aren't harming the earth.

Or think about some other specialties:

- Caring for antiques
- Caring for hardwood floors
- Cleaning for those with allergies, asthma, or other health issues

- Working with real estate agents or apartment managers to clean homes on the market
- Working with event planners to offer before- or after-party cleaning
- Combining housecleaning services with house- or pet-sitting, dog walking, errand running, lawn care, gourmet cooking, car washing, gift buying, interior decorating—anything you like

It's *your* business, and you can take it in whatever direction you like.

We hope this book has offered you some ideas, information, and inspiration as you start up your own home-based housecleaning business. You have a lot of very hard work ahead of you, but the process can be more rewarding than you ever imagined. We wish you the very best!

Appendix I

Checklist of Start-Up Requirements

You might not need all of these items right away, but it's a good idea to have them in mind as you start up your business.

- ☐ Business license
- ☐ Fictitious name registration
- ☐ Liability insurance
- ☐ Bonding insurance
- ☐ Computer and accessories
- ☐ Internet service provider
- ☐ Business telephone line
- ☐ Telephone and voice mail system
- ☐ Desk or table
- ☐ Chair
- ☐ File cabinets
- ☐ Fireproof safe
- ☐ Basic office supplies
- ☐ Basic cleaning supplies
- ☐ Vacuum cleaner
- ☐ Newspaper advertising
- ☐ Business checking account
- ☐ Merchant account
- ☐ Graphic designer for logo

Appendix II

Resources

Where to Get Your Business Questions Answered

Small Business Administration (SBA)
(800) UASK–SBA
Fax (202) 205–7064
www.sba.gov
answerdesk@sba.gov
For local offices of the SBA, check in your phone book under "U.S. Government" or visit the Web site.

The SBA is a terrific resource for business owners and potential owners, and it's free. At offices (called Small Business Development Centers or Business Information Centers) across the country, you can sign up for free training programs; receive free one-on-one counseling on everything from applying for a business license to paying taxes; and receive free publications on all aspects of starting, expanding, and operating your business. (These publications can also be downloaded from the SBA's Web site.) There are special programs for women in business, for socially and economically disadvantaged businesses, for veterans, and much more. (Two of these programs that may be especially useful are listed below.) Financial assistance in the form of individual counseling, loan application walk-throughs, and loan guaranties and disaster assistance is also available. Did we mention that it's free?

Service Corps of Retired Executives (SCORE)

www.score.org (or contact your local office of the SBA)

SCORE, a resource partner with the SBA, is an all-volunteer nonprofit organization dedicated solely to helping small businesses succeed. Retired executives and business owners from all walks of life offer their knowledge as a community service. These folks know what they're doing, and they're dedicated to helping you. You can receive e-mail counseling or one-on-one counseling through local offices, or sign up for workshops and training. SCORE's Web site is also full of helpful information and links to every business resource you can imagine.

Office of Women's Business Ownership

Small Business Administration

409 Third Street SW, Fourth Floor

Washington, DC 20416

(202) 205–6673

www.onlinewbc.gov

owbo@sba.gov

Women business owners often face unique issues, and this organization can help you navigate your way through them all. You'll find workshops, roundtables, and one-on-one counseling opportunities to help you open, license, finance, and expand your business. The Online Women's Business Center Web site is helpful and inspiring.

Internal Revenue Service

www.irs.gov

(800) 829–1040 (for information or tax questions)

(800) 829–4059 (TTY/TDD)

(800) 829–3676 (to order forms, instructions, and publications)

Western U.S.

Western Area Distribution Center

Rancho Cordova, CA 95743-0001

Central U.S.
Central Area Distribution Center
P.O. Box 8903
Bloomington, IL 61702-8903

Eastern U.S. and foreign addresses
Eastern Area Distribution Center
P.O. Box 85074
Richmond, VA 23261-5074

Yes, we know, the idea of contacting the IRS voluntarily is a little intimidating. It can be done, and in fact the IRS has made good on its recent pledges to become a "kinder, gentler" organization. The Web site is a good place to start. There's a Small Business Corner for information, and answers to frequently asked questions. You can download any form you might ever need, as well as dozens of publications. In particular, you might want to check out

- Publication 583, *Starting a Business and Keeping Records* (includes sample forms)
- Publication 587, *Business Use of Your Home*
- Publication 910, *Guide to Free Tax Services*
- Publication 1546, *The Taxpayer Advocate Service of the IRS*
- Publication 3207, *Small Business Resource Guide* (an interactive CD-ROM)
- You can also request these by mail or phone.

Where to Get Your Housecleaning Questions Answered

The Internet
The World Wide Web offers a stunning amount of information on cleaning. Take advantage of others' knowledge and experience by typing *cleaning tips* or *housecleaning* into a search engine. You'll have hundreds of thousands of sites to choose from, with everything from cleaning products for sale to enormous lists of tips for cleaning things you never even realized needed cleaning (bowling balls?). Many sites also offer e-mail connections so that you can contact the experts with your housecleaning questions. Some provide hot lines you

can call when you're stumped. There are also newsgroups and forums where you can search other people's cleaning ideas, add your own, and discuss cleaning issues on-line. Do take everything on the Net with a grain of salt, however. You'll find fantastic advice, but you'll also find information from questionable sources, along with come-ons, scams, and brazen product hawking.

Books

There are a lot of good books on the market with all sorts of housecleaning tips—everything from removing stains to improving efficiency. Most of these are geared toward helping people clean their own homes, but you can tweak the information to suit your own needs. Here's just a small sampling.

Aslett, Don. *The Cleaning Encyclopedia: Your A to Z Illustrated Guide to Cleaning Like the Pros.* New York: Dell Publishing, 1993.

Bredenberg, Jeff, ed. *Clean It Fast, Clean It Right: The Ultimate Guide to Making Absolutely Everything You Own Sparkle and Shine.* Emmaus, Penn.: Rodale Press, 1998.

Both *The Cleaning Encyclopedia* and *Clean It Fast, Clean It Right* offer alphabetical listings describing how to clean just about every item or stain you can imagine, along with information about cleaning supplies and equipment. If you're ever presented with a thorny cleaning question (and clients will ask you about everything, from how to clean acoustical tile to how to remove chipmunk blood from velvet), these books can help you cope like the expert you are. Both make for livelier reading than you might expect.

Campbell, Jeff, and the Clean Team. *Speed Cleaning.* 3d ed. New York: Dell Publishing, 1991.

Jeff Campbell and the Clean Team (a California-based housecleaning service) offer a complete line of housecleaning resources, including several other books, a cleaning products catalog, a Web site (www.thecleanteam.com), and even a hot line you can call with cleaning questions (800–238–2996). *Speed Cleaning* outlines a detailed method for cleaning houses as efficiently as possible. Whether you adapt all of the Clean Team's program or not, the book has some good tips, especially on time management and environmentally friendly cleaning.

Appendix III

Blank Room Plans

One of the most important things you can do for yourself as you embark on your house-cleaning career is to come to a clear understanding with your clients about exactly what services you will perform. Put this understanding in writing before you dust a single countertop! You and your clients will then know exactly what to expect.

The room plans that follow are designed to help you get started with this kind of planning. Bring them along on consultations or use them as models to create room plans of your own, adapting them to fit your needs.

Client: _____　　　　**Room: Vestibule**

Floor Finish

Wood _____　Carpet _____　Tile _____

Other _____

Wall Finish

Wood paneling _____　　Tile _____　　Paint over plaster _____

Washable wallpaper over plaster _____　　Wood wainscoting _____

Plastic wainscoting _____　　Other _____

Entrance Door

Wood _____　Metal _____

Door windows _____

Miscellaneous Tasks

ETT: _____ Minutes (Vestibule)

Client: _____   **Room: Living Room**

Floor Finish

Wood _____   Carpet _____   Tile _____

Other _____

Wall Finish

Wood paneling _____   Tile _____   Paint over plaster _____

Washable wallpaper over plaster _____   Wood wainscoting _____

Plastic wainscoting _____   Other _____

Appliances

Televison _____   VCR _____   Stereo component unit _____   Humidifier _____

Other _____

Other Furnishings

Coffee table _____   Bookcase _____   End table _____   Paintings _____

Metal and glass lamp fixtures _____

Miscellaneous _____

Miscellaneous Tasks

ETT: _____ Minutes (Living Room)

Client: _____   **Room: Dining Room**

Floor Finish

Wood _____ Carpet _____ Tile _____

Other _____

Wall Finish

Wood paneling _____   Tile _____   Paint over plaster _____

Washable wallpaper over plaster _____   Wood wainscoting _____

Plastic wainscoting _____   Other _____

Table

Wood _____ Glass _____ Acrylic _____

Other _____

Chairs

Wood _____ Upholstered _____ Other _____

Other Furnishings

Buffet _____

Breakfront _____

Bar _____

Light fixtures _____

Paintings _____

Miscellaneous _____

Miscellaneous Tasks

ETT: _____ Minutes (Dining Room)

Client: _____   **Room: Family Room**

Floor Finish

Wood _____ Carpet _____ Tile _____

Other _____

Wall Finish

Wood paneling _____   Tile _____   Paint over plaster _____

Washable wallpaper over plaster _____   Wood wainscoting _____

Plastic wainscoting _____   Other _____

Appliances

Televison _____ VCR _____ Stereo component unit _____ Humidifier _____

Other _____

Other Furnishings

Coffee table _____ Bookcase _____ End table _____ Paintings _____

Metal and glass lamp fixtures _____

Miscellaneous _____

Miscellaneous Tasks

ETT: _____ Minutes (Family Room)

Client: _____   **Room: Den**

Floor Finish

Wood _____   Carpet _____   Tile _____

Other _____

Wall Finish

Wood paneling _____   Tile _____   Paint over plaster _____

Washable wallpaper over plaster _____   Wood wainscoting _____

Plastic wainscoting _____   Other _____

Appliances

Televison _____   VCR _____   Stereo component unit _____   Humidifier _____

Other _____

Other Furnishings

Coffee table _____   Bookcase _____   End table _____   Paintings _____

Metal and glass lamp fixtures _____

Miscellaneous _____

Miscellaneous Tasks

ETT: _____ Minutes (Den)

Client: _____   **Room: Office**

Floor Finish

Wood _____   Carpet _____   Tile _____

Other _____

Wall Finish

Wood paneling _____   Tile _____   Paint over plaster _____

Washable wallpaper over plaster _____   Wood wainscoting _____

Plastic wainscoting _____   Other _____

Appliances

Televison _____   VCR _____   Stereo component unit _____   Humidifier _____

Other _____

Other Furnishings

Coffee table _____   Bookcase _____   End table _____   Paintings _____

Metal and glass lamp fixtures _____

Miscellaneous _____

Miscellaneous Tasks

ETT: _____ Minutes (Office)

Client: _____   **Room: Stairway 1**

Floor Finish

Wood _____   Carpet _____   Tile _____

Other _____

Wall Finish

Wood paneling _____   Tile _____   Paint over plaster _____

Washable wallpaper over plaster _____   Wood wainscoting _____

Plastic wainscoting _____   Other _____

Miscellaneous Tasks

ETT: _____ Minutes (Stairway 1)

Client: _____   **Room: Stairway 2**

Floor Finish

Wood _____   Carpet _____   Tile _____

Other _____

Wall Finish

Wood paneling _____   Tile _____   Paint over plaster _____

Washable wallpaper over plaster _____   Wood wainscoting _____

Plastic wainscoting _____   Other _____

Miscellaneous Tasks

ETT: _____ Minutes (Stairway 2)

Client: _____   **Room: Kitchen**

Floor Finish

Wood _____   Carpet _____   Tile _____

Other _____

Wall Finish

Wood paneling _____   Tile _____   Paint over plaster _____

Washable wallpaper over plaster _____   Wood wainscoting _____

Plastic wainscoting _____   Other _____

Countertop

Wood _____   Fiberglass _____   Tile _____

Other _____

Sink

Porcelain _____   Acrylic _____   Stainless steel _____

Other _____

Appliances

Stove _____   Garbage disposal _____   Dishwasher _____

Refrigerator _____   Trash compactor _____   Microwave oven _____

Toaster oven _____   Other _____

Miscellaneous Tasks

ETT: _____ Minutes (Kitchen)

Client: _____   **Room: Bathroom 1**

Floor
Laminate _____   Tile _____   Marble _____

Other _____

Tub/Shower
Fiberglass _____   Porcelain _____   Ceramic tile _____

Other _____

Toilet

Walls
Wooden wainscoting _____   Painted plaster _____   Tile _____

Other _____

Vanity
Porcelain _____   Stainless steel _____   Acrylic _____   Formica _____

Wood _____   Glass _____   Chrome _____

Other _____

Door
Wood _____   Glass _____   Other _____

Towel Rack and Wall Decorations
Chrome _____   Wood _____   Acrylic _____   Glass _____

Other _____

Miscellaneous Tasks

ETT: _____ Minutes (Bathroom 1)

Client: _____   **Room: Bathroom 2**

Floor

Laminate _____   Tile _____   Marble _____

Other _____

Tub/Shower

Fiberglass _____   Porcelain _____   Ceramic tile _____

Other _____

Toilet

Walls

Wooden wainscoting _____   Painted plaster _____   Tile _____

Other _____

Vanity

Porcelain _____   Stainless steel _____   Acrylic _____   Formica _____

Wood _____   Glass _____   Chrome _____

Other _____

Door

Wood _____   Glass _____   Other _____

Towel Rack and Wall Decorations

Chrome _____   Wood _____   Acrylic _____   Glass _____

Other _____

Miscellaneous Tasks

ETT: _____ Minutes (Bathroom 2)

Client: _____   **Room: Bathroom 3**

Floor

Laminate _____   Tile _____   Marble _____

Other _____

Tub/Shower

Fiberglass _____   Porcelain _____   Ceramic tile _____

Other _____

Toilet

Walls

Wooden wainscoting _____   Painted plaster _____   Tile _____

Other _____

Vanity

Porcelain _____   Stainless steel _____   Acrylic _____   Formica _____

Wood _____   Glass _____   Chrome _____

Other _____

Door

Wood _____   Glass _____   Other _____

Towel Rack and Wall Decorations

Chrome _____   Wood _____   Acrylic _____   Glass _____

Other _____

Miscellaneous Tasks

ETT: _____ Minutes (Bathroom 3)

Appendix III

Client: _____   **Room: Bedroom 1**

Floor

Wood _____   Carpet _____   Tile _____

Other _____

Nightstand and Dresser

Wood _____   Glass _____   Acrylic _____

Other _____

Other Furnishings

Miscellaneous Tasks

ETT: _____ Minutes (Bedroom 1)

Client: _____   **Room: Bedroom 2**

Floor

Wood _____   Carpet _____   Tile _____

Other _____

Nightstand and Dresser

Wood _____   Glass _____   Acrylic _____

Other _____

Other Furnishings

Miscellaneous Tasks

ETT: _____ Minutes (Bedroom 2)

Client: _____   **Room: Bedroom 3**

Floor

Wood _____   Carpet _____   Tile _____

Other _____

Nightstand and Dresser

Wood _____   Glass _____   Acrylic _____

Other _____

Other Furnishings

Miscellaneous Tasks

ETT: _____ Minutes (Bedroom 3)

Client: _____   **Room: Bedroom 4**

Floor

Wood _____   Carpet _____   Tile _____

Other _____

Nightstand and Dresser

Wood _____   Glass _____   Acrylic _____

Other _____

Other Furnishings

Miscellaneous Tasks

ETT: _____ Minutes (Bedroom 1)

Client: _____   **Room: Laundry Room**

Floor

Cement _____ Wood _____ Carpet _____ Tile _____
Other _____

Metal Appliances

Washer _____ Dryer _____

Utility Sink

Acrylic _____ Stainless steel _____ Other _____

Miscellaneous Tasks

ETT: _____ minutes (Laundry Room)

Client: _____ **Other Room:** _____

Floor

Wood _____ Carpet _____ Tile _____

Other _____

Wall Finish

Wood paneling _____ Tile _____ Paint over plaster _____

Washable wallpaper over plaster _____ Wood wainscoting _____

Plastic wainscoting _____ Other _____

Furnishings

Miscellaneous Tasks

ETT: _____ Minutes (Other Room)

Home Plan: _____

Vestibule:	_____	minutes
Living Room:	_____	minutes
Dining Room:	_____	minutes
Family Room:	_____	minutes
Den:	_____	minutes
Office:	_____	minutes
Stairway 1:	_____	minutes
Stairway 2:	_____	minutes
Kitchen:	_____	minutes
Bathroom 1:	_____	minutes
Bathroom 2:	_____	minutes
Bathroom 3:	_____	minutes
Bedroom 1:	_____	minutes
Bedroom 2:	_____	minutes
Bedroom 3:	_____	minutes
Bedroom 4:	_____	minutes
Laundry Room:	_____	minutes
Other Room:	_____	minutes

Total time: _____

Charge: _____